TUBULARS

D. L. De McClung

Copyright © 2019 D. L. De McClung

All rights reserved.

ISBN: 9781792702617

<o>

Re'el De'el Books
Eye Demon Studios
McClung Originals
~
D'eldeli Los Festus on Teverbaugh
Worthington WV 26591
America

DEDICATION

To
My dear departed mother who didn't always understand me or what it was I did
but loved me anyway.
1926-2018

Other books by D. L. De McClung

WORDS IN A ROW: BOOK ONE
[The early poems]

WORDS IN A ROW: BOOK TWO
[Current and recent poems]

SQUARISMS
[A digital art project]

LINEARISMS
[A digital art project]

FLOWERS DE' ART
[Flower pictures with poems]

COLORS
[A digital art project]

OF A WOMAN
[Artistic nude shots]

NIPS
[A celebration of the human nipple]

SHE WAS THEIR MEAT
[A sexually explicit epic poem]

The official website of the Artist D. L. De McClung:
deldemcclung.com

De McClung's podcast:
spreaker.com/show/de-mcclungs-art-ra-monologs

De McClung's page on fineartamerica.com:
de-mcclung.pixels.com

De McClung's WebStore:
deldemcclung.com/products-page/

Look for De McClung's Art on:
RedBubble.com

Check out De McClung's Channel on:
YouTube.com

Follow De McClung on Facebook:
https://www.facebook.com/oculus.dar

Follow De McClung on Google Plus:
https://plus.google.com/+DeMcClung

Follow De McClung on Twitter:
@deelmcclung

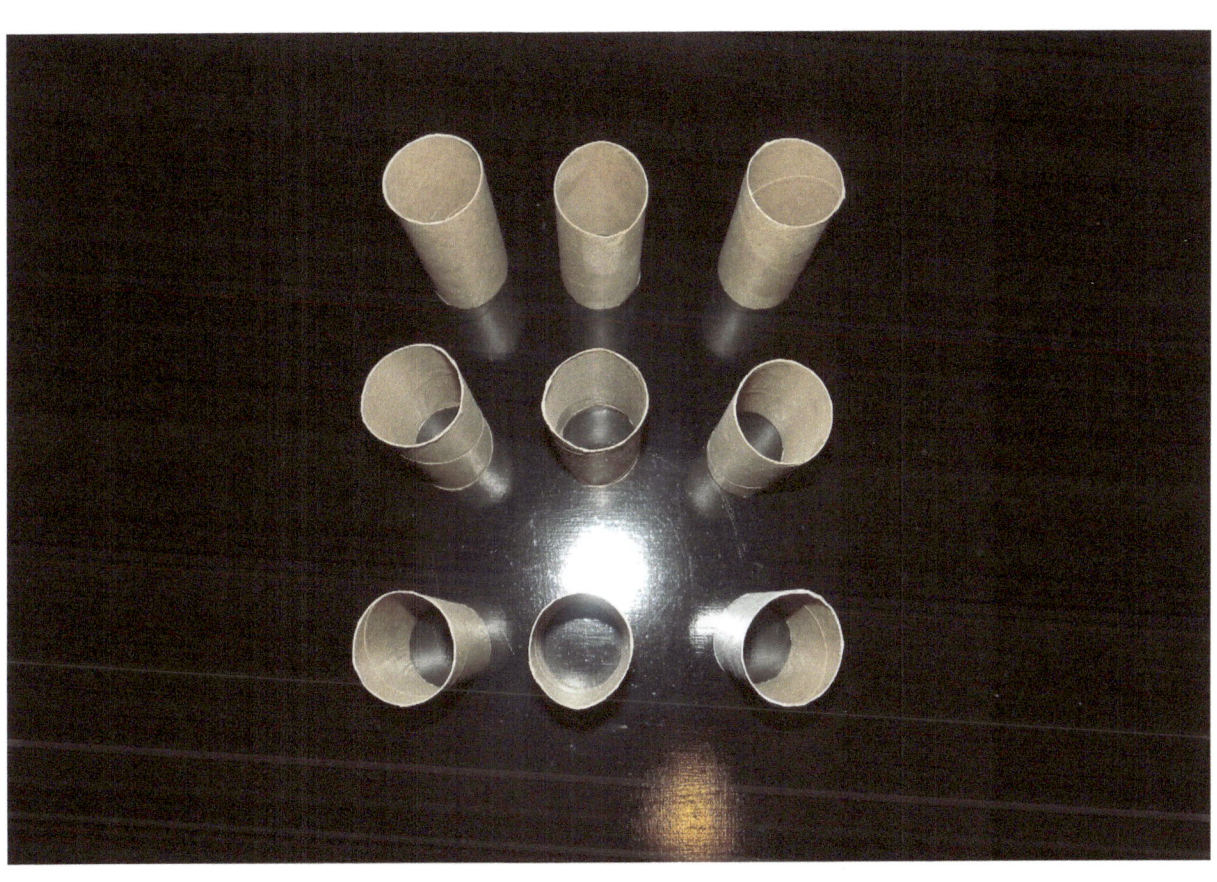

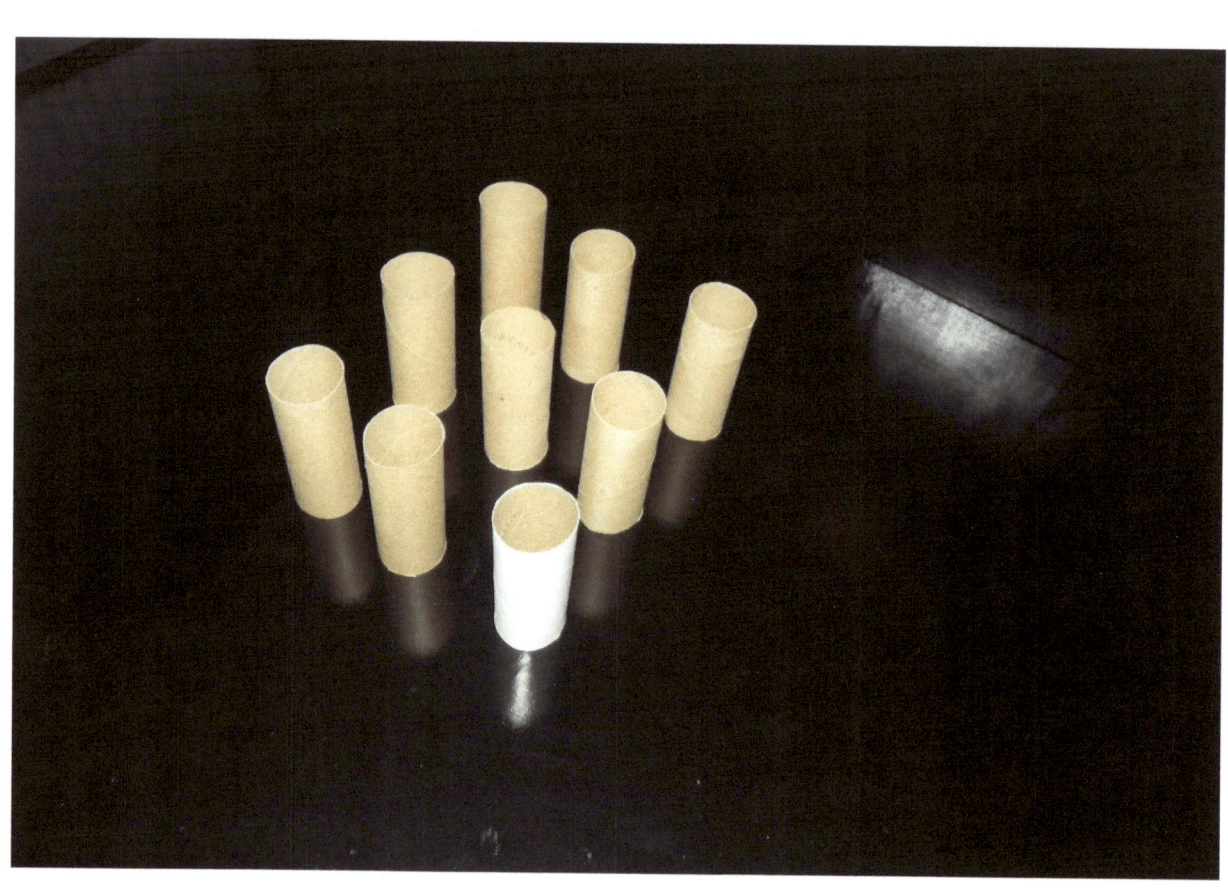

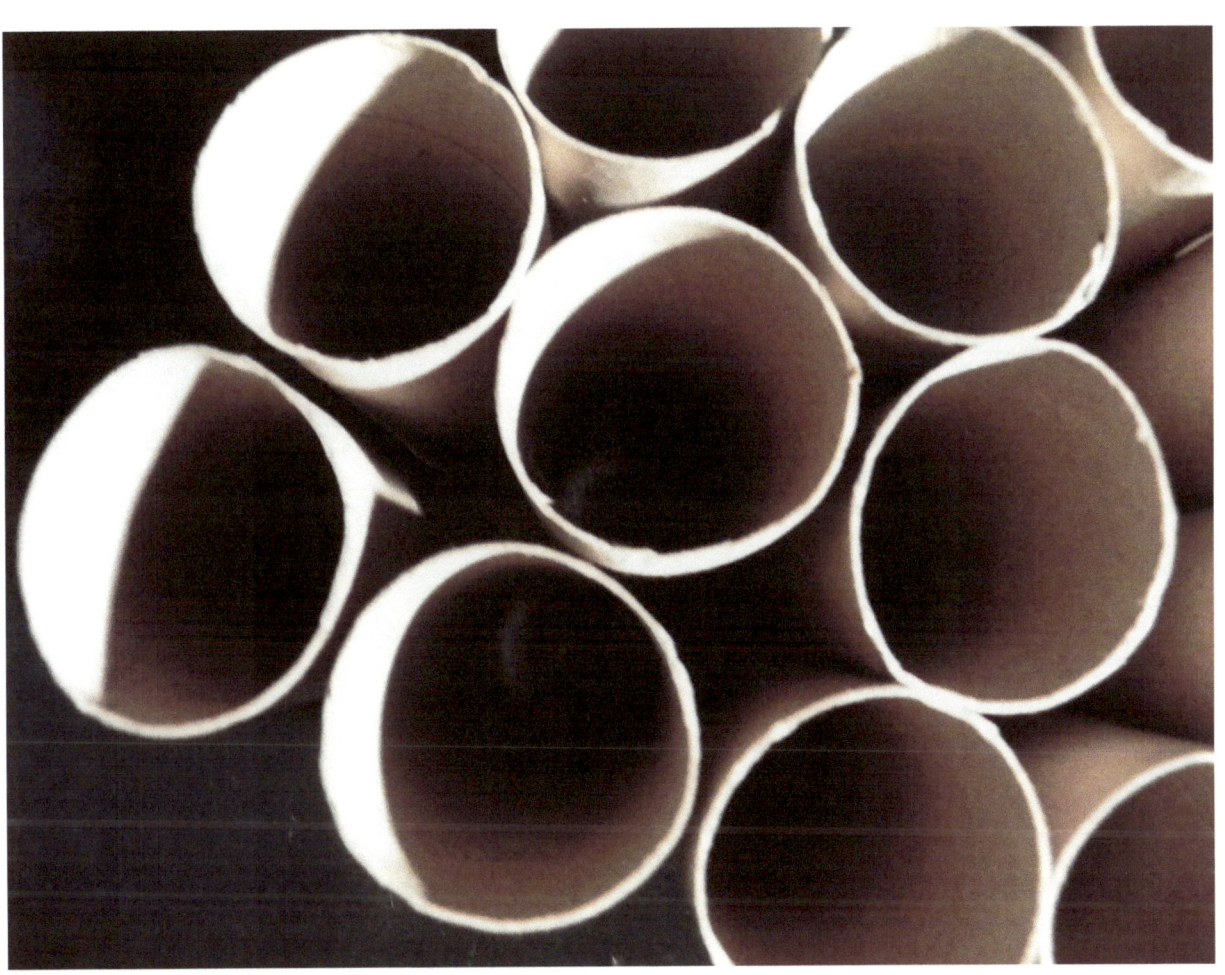

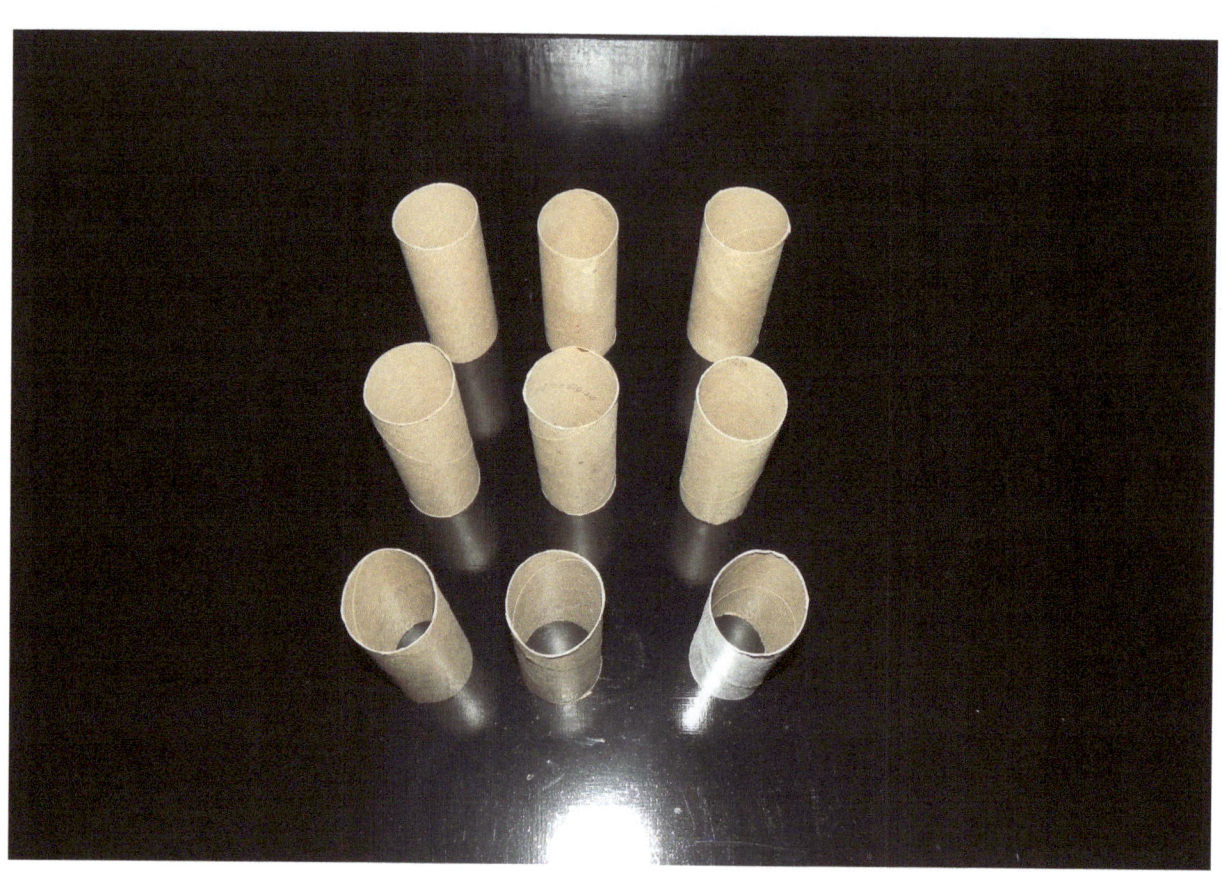

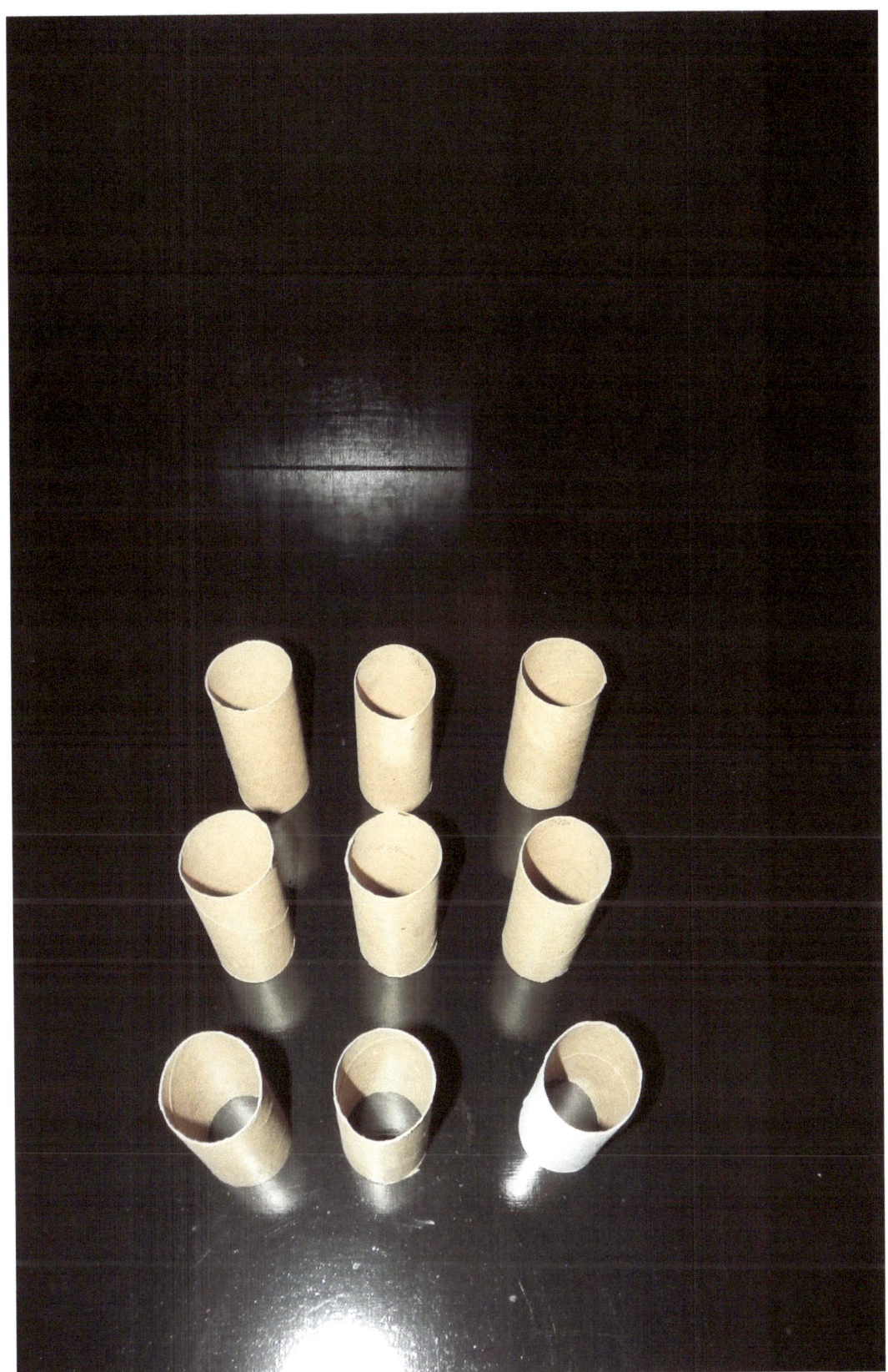

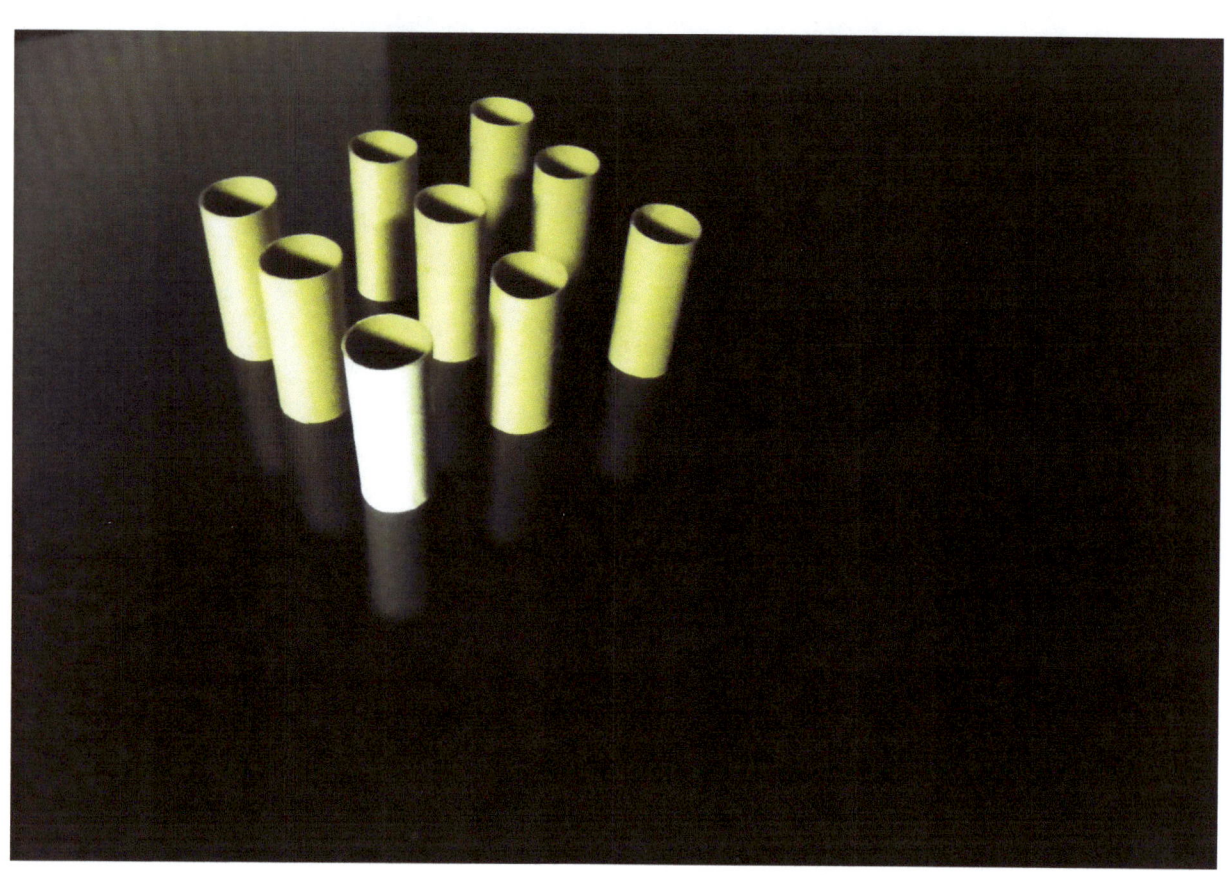

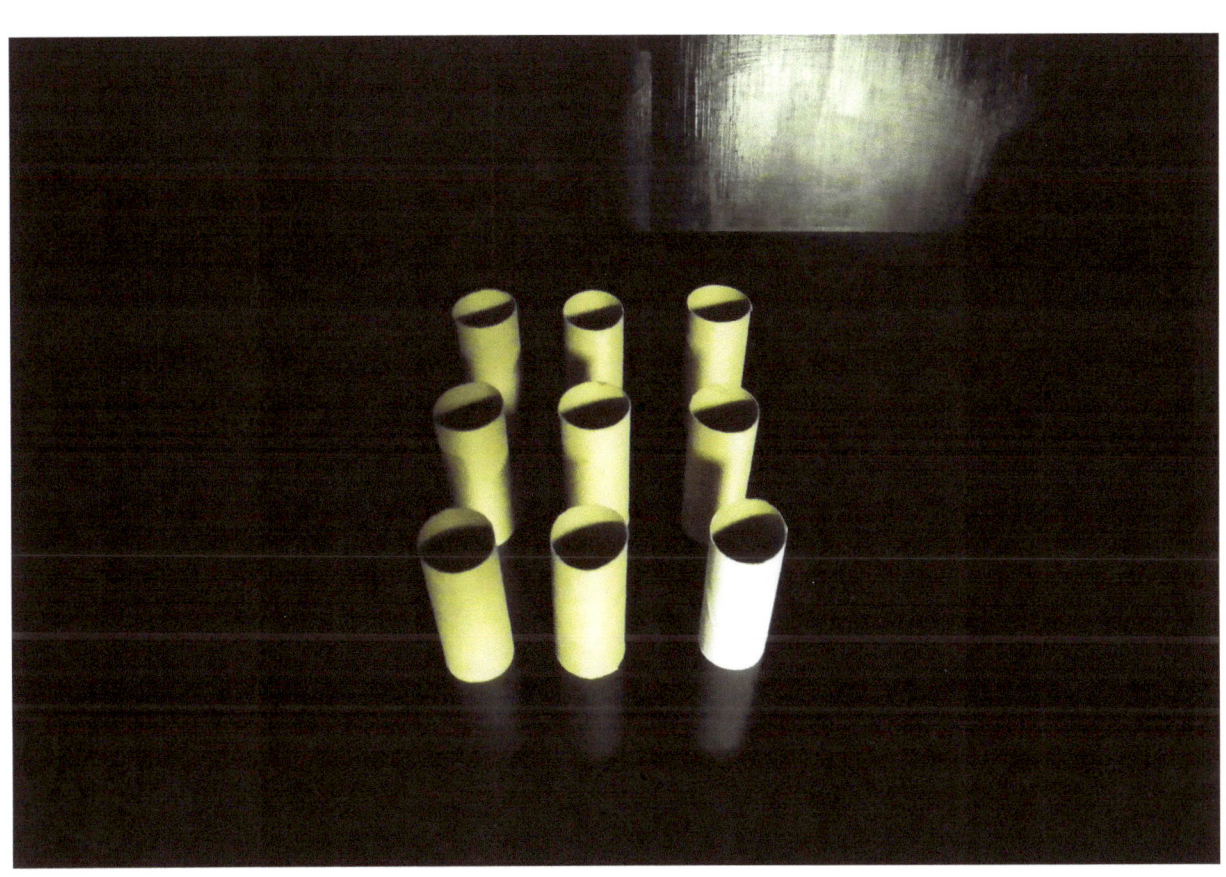

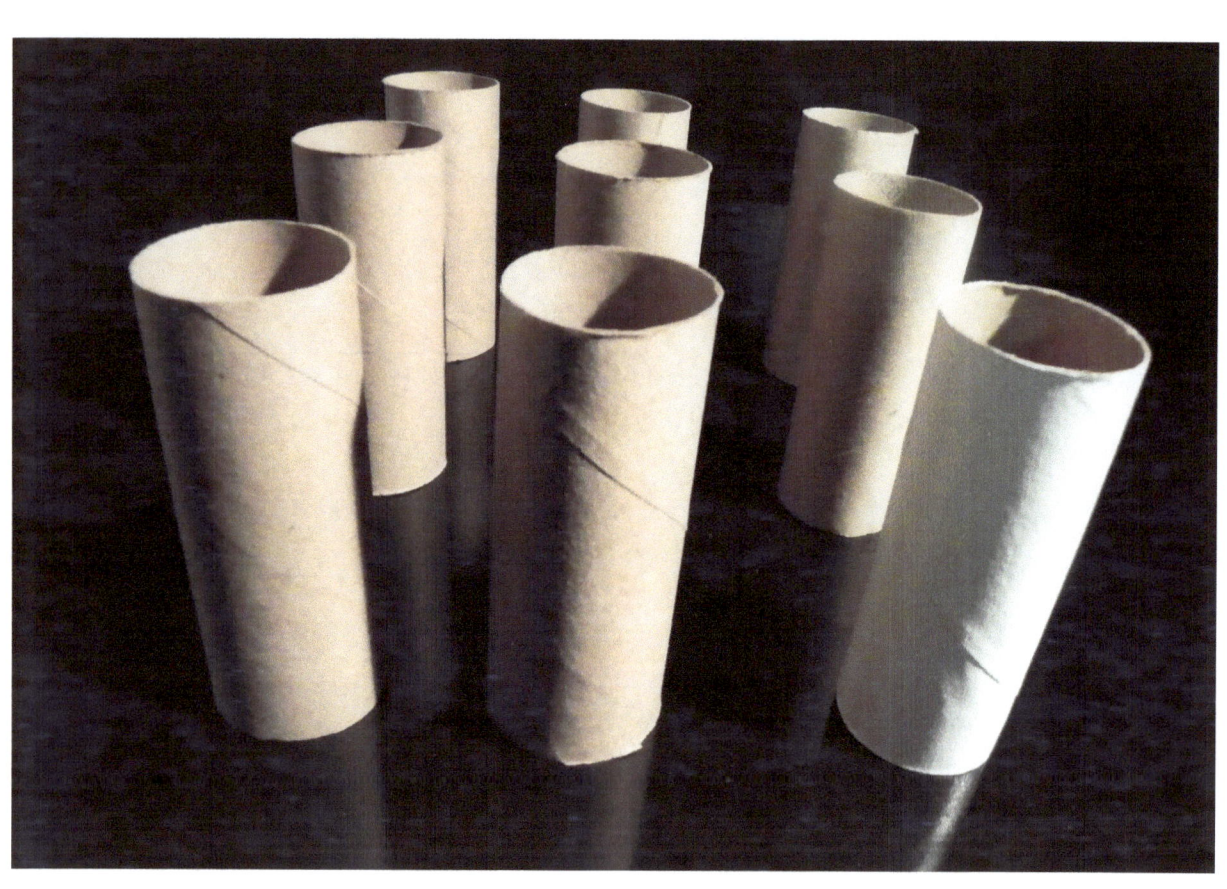

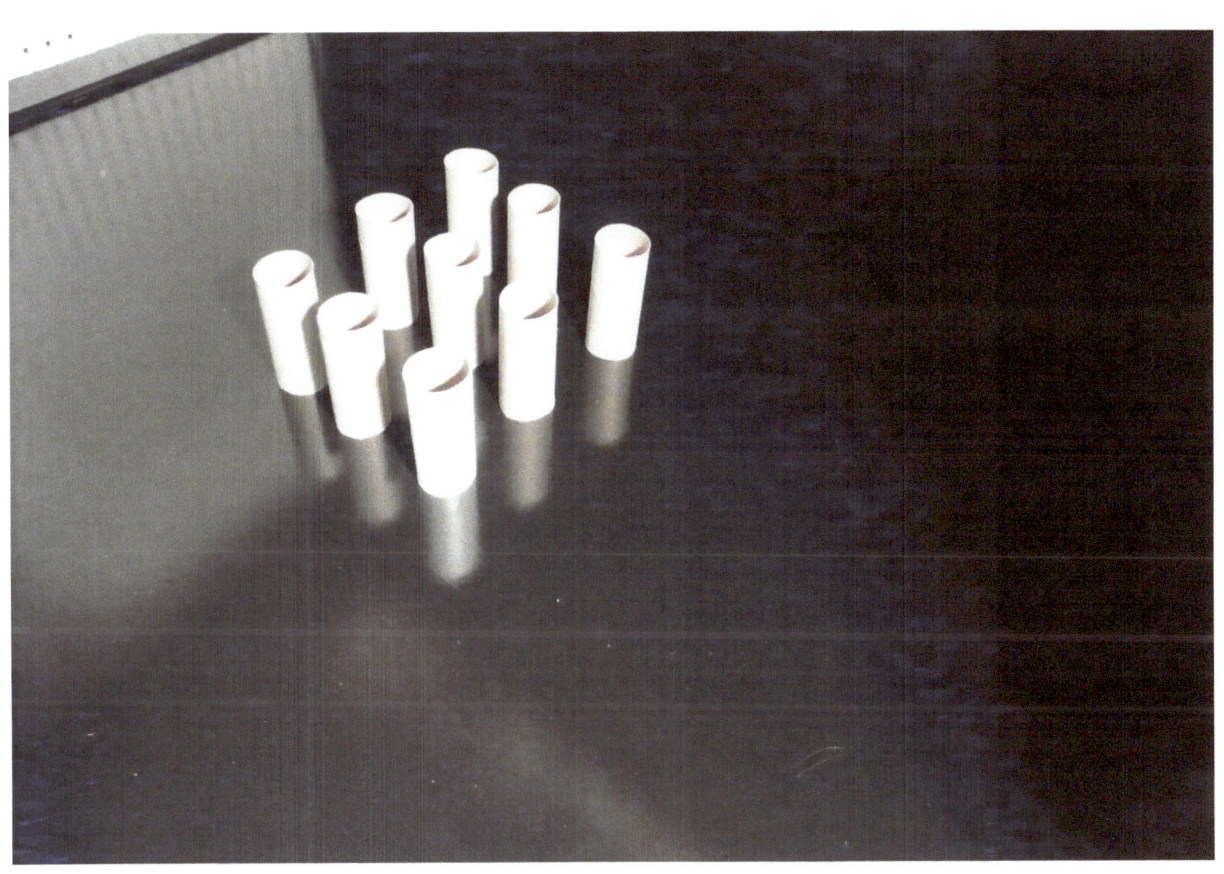

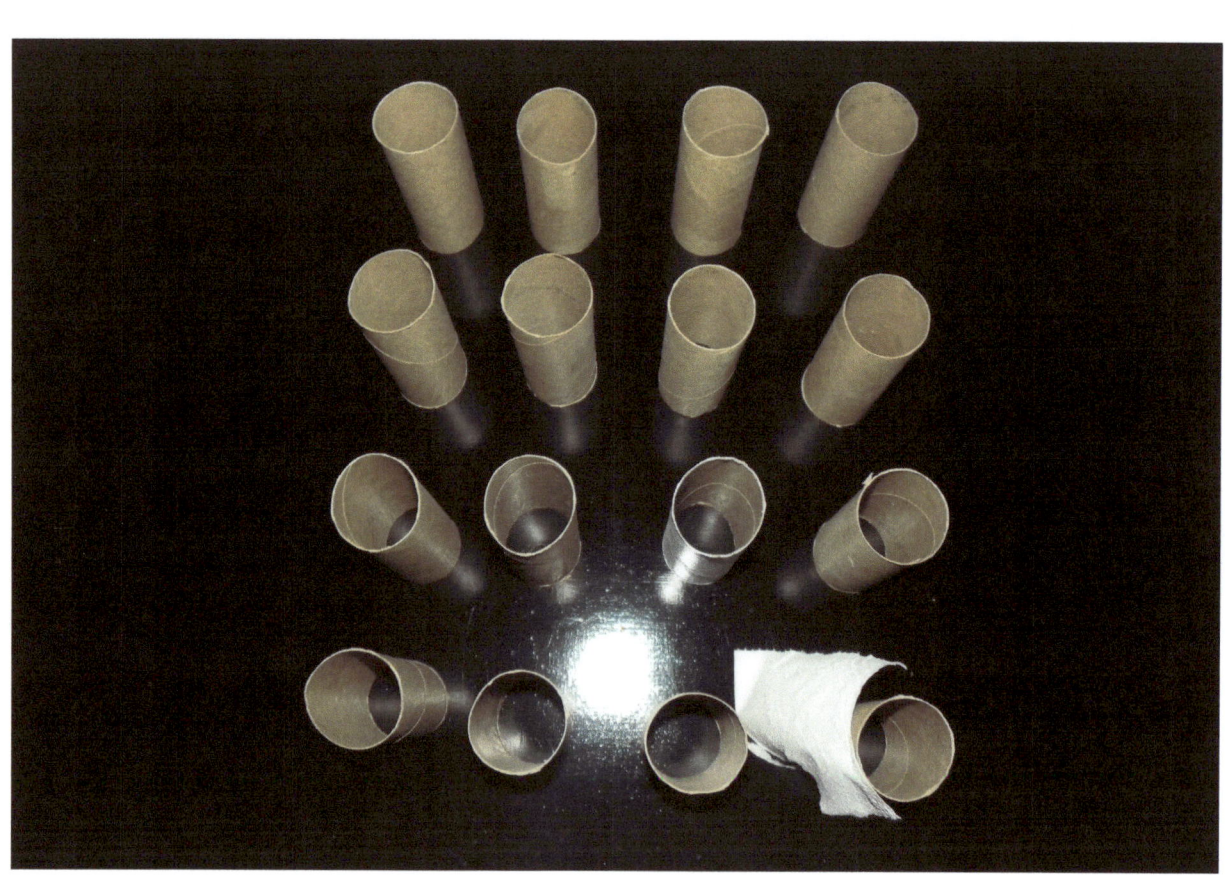

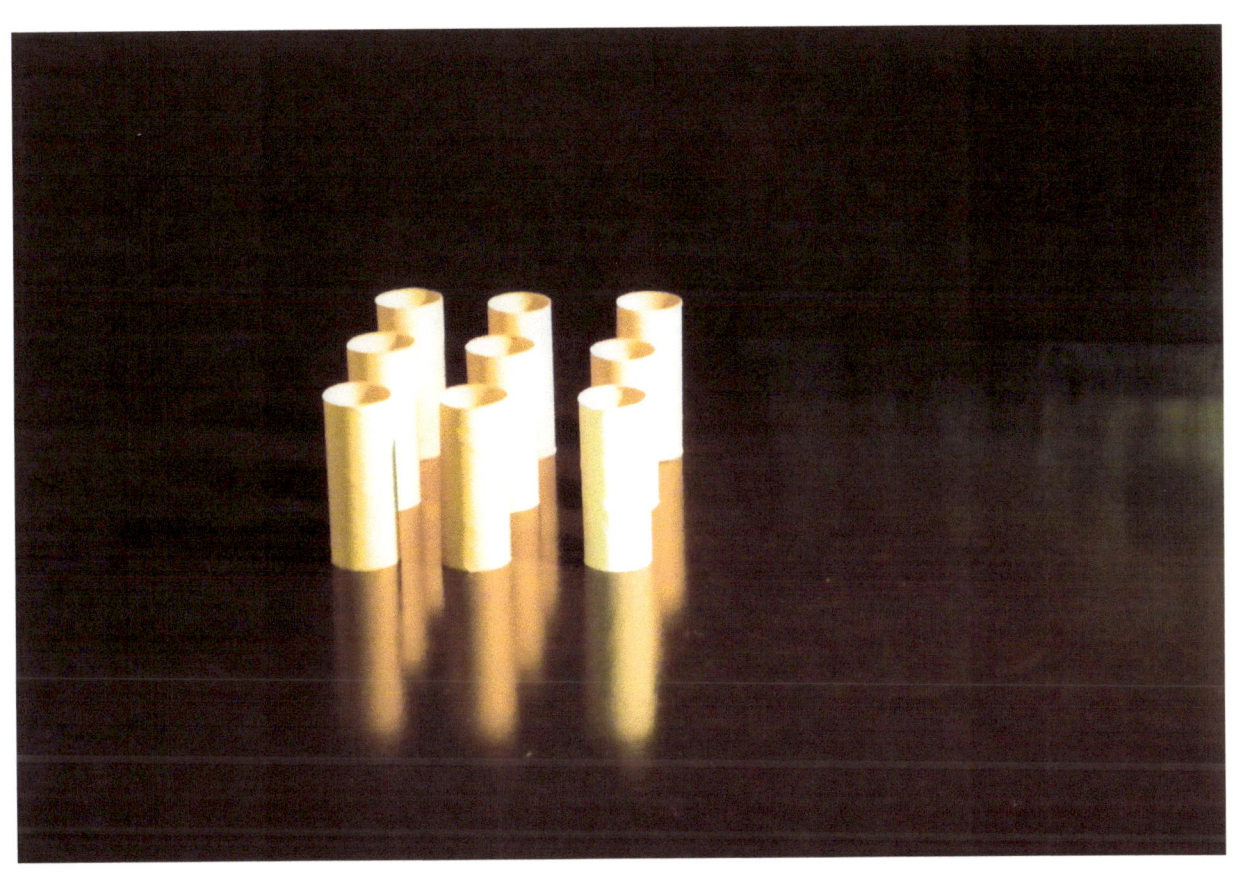

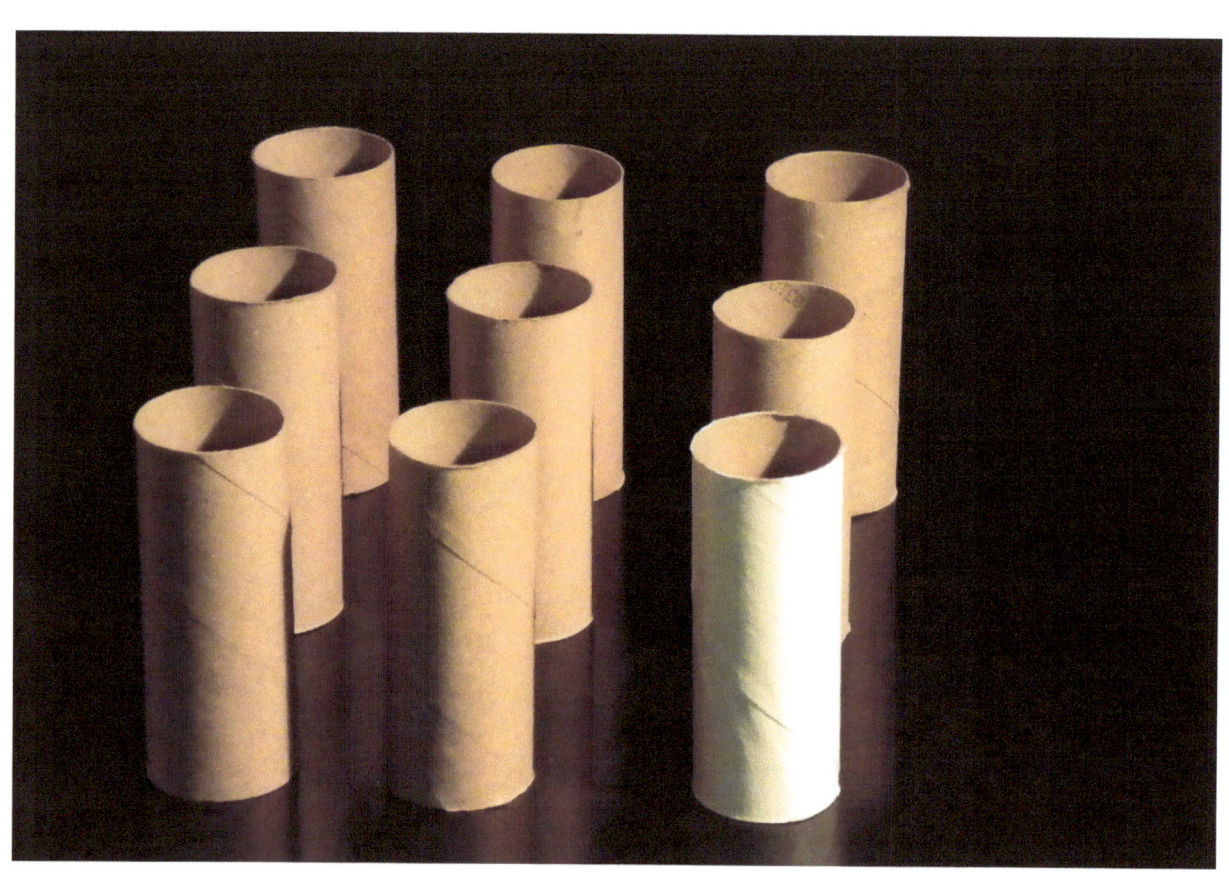

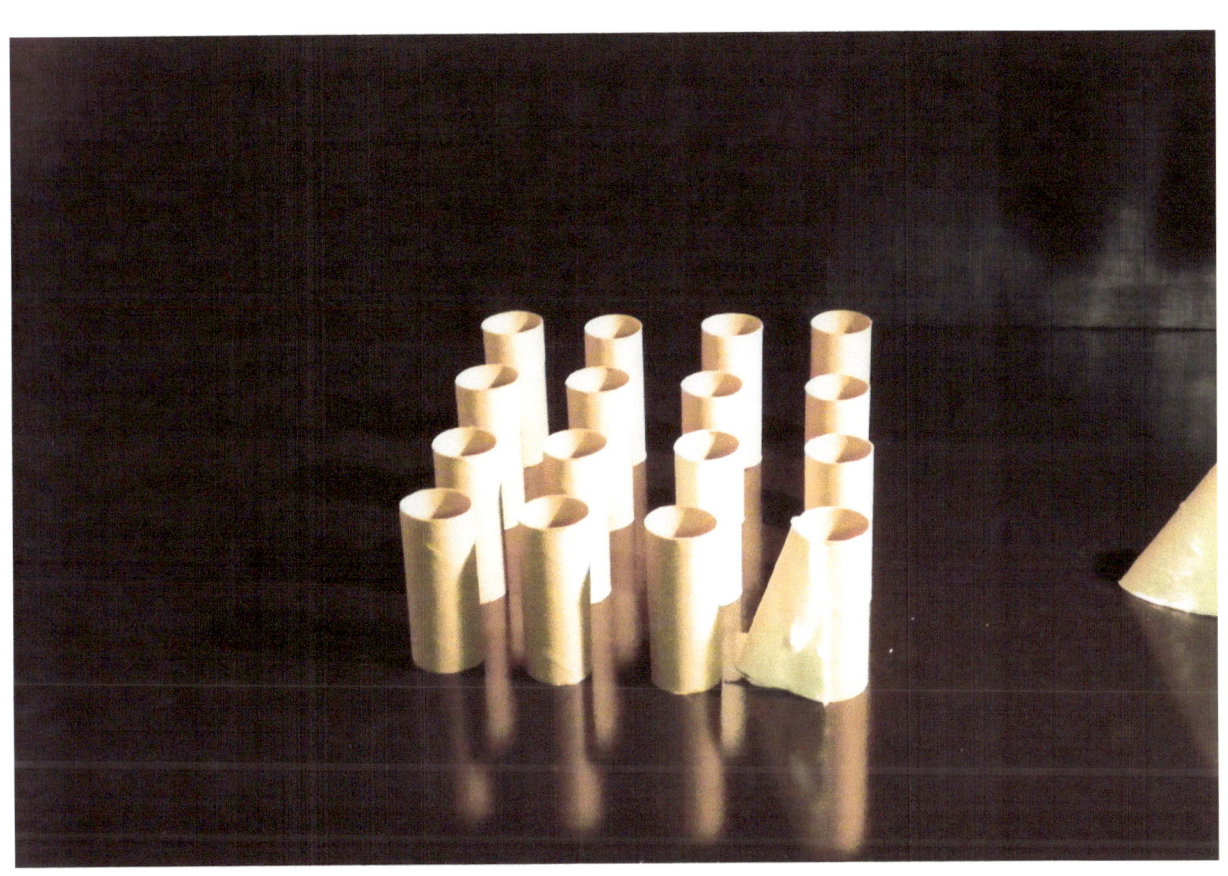

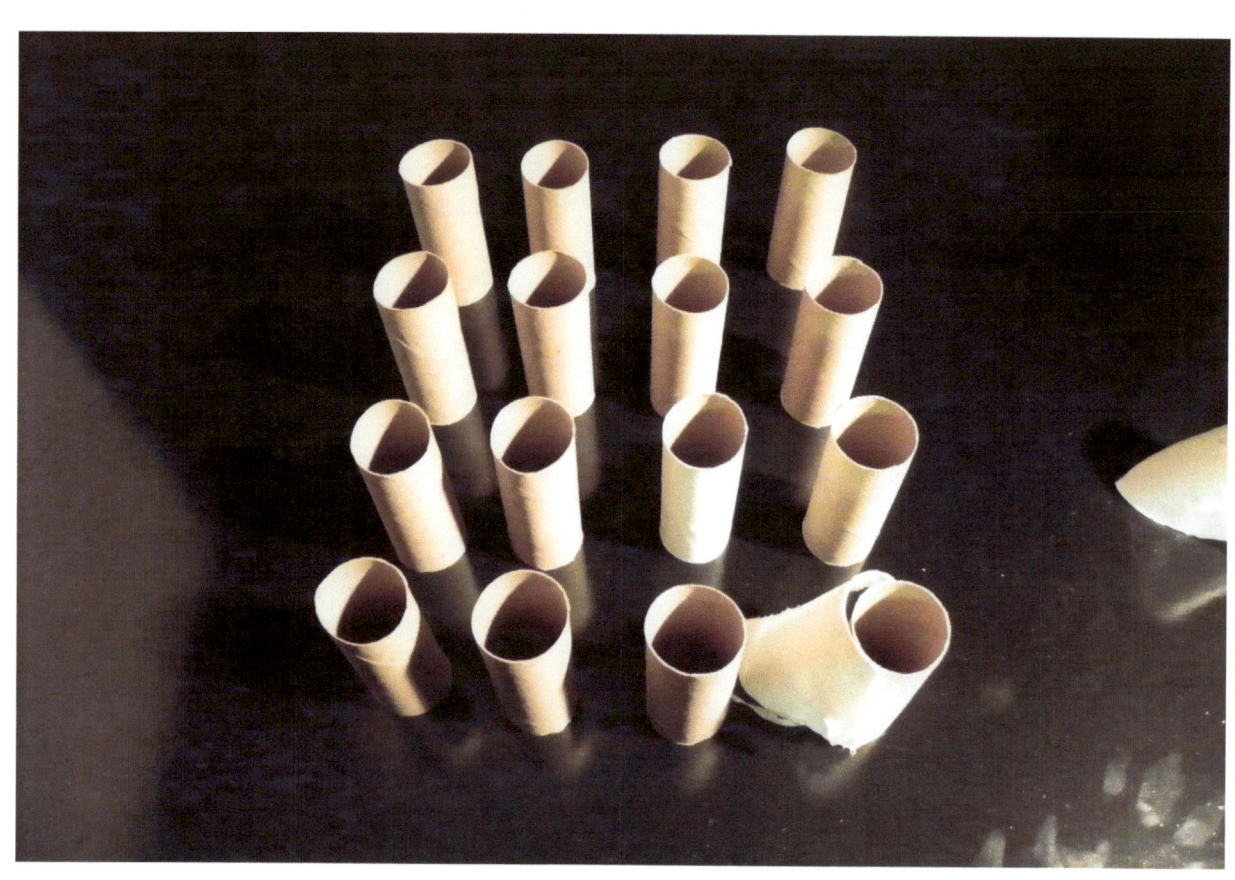

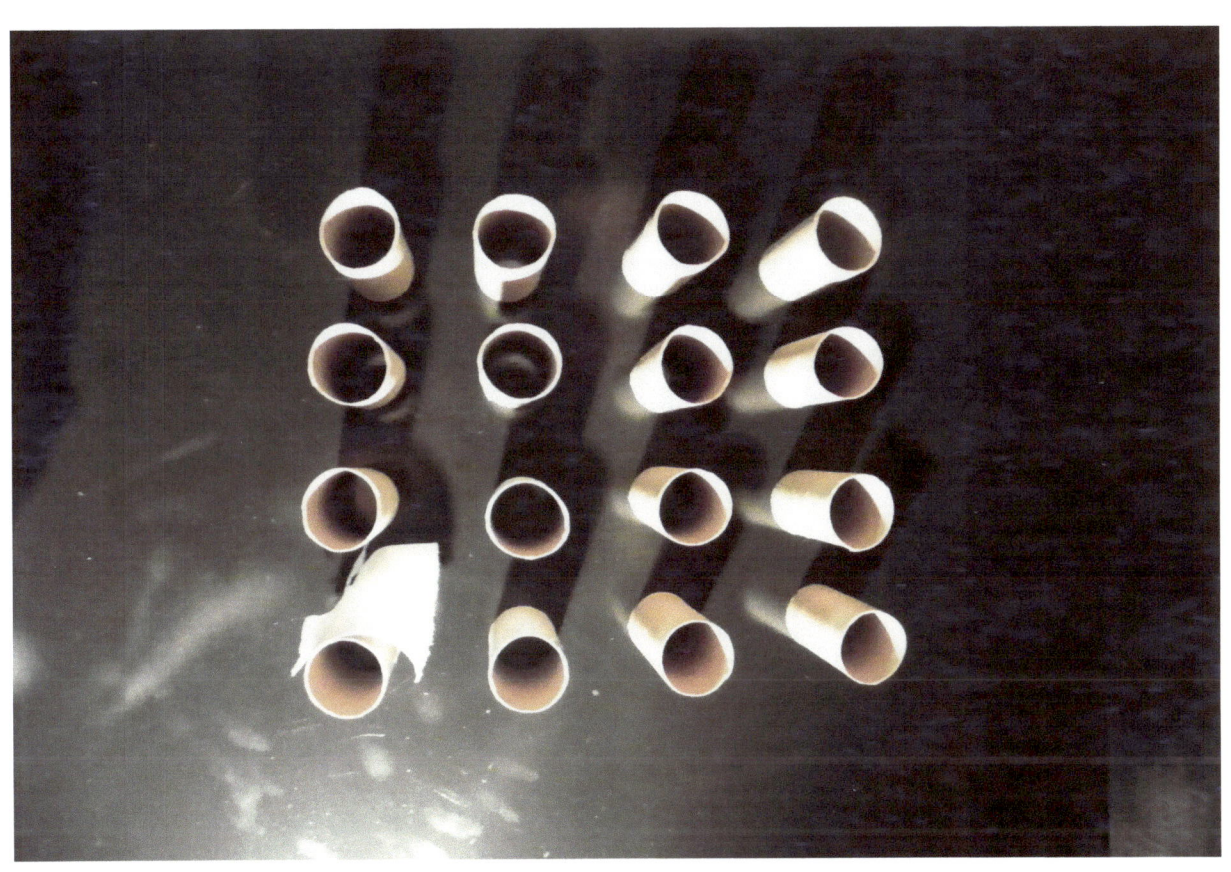

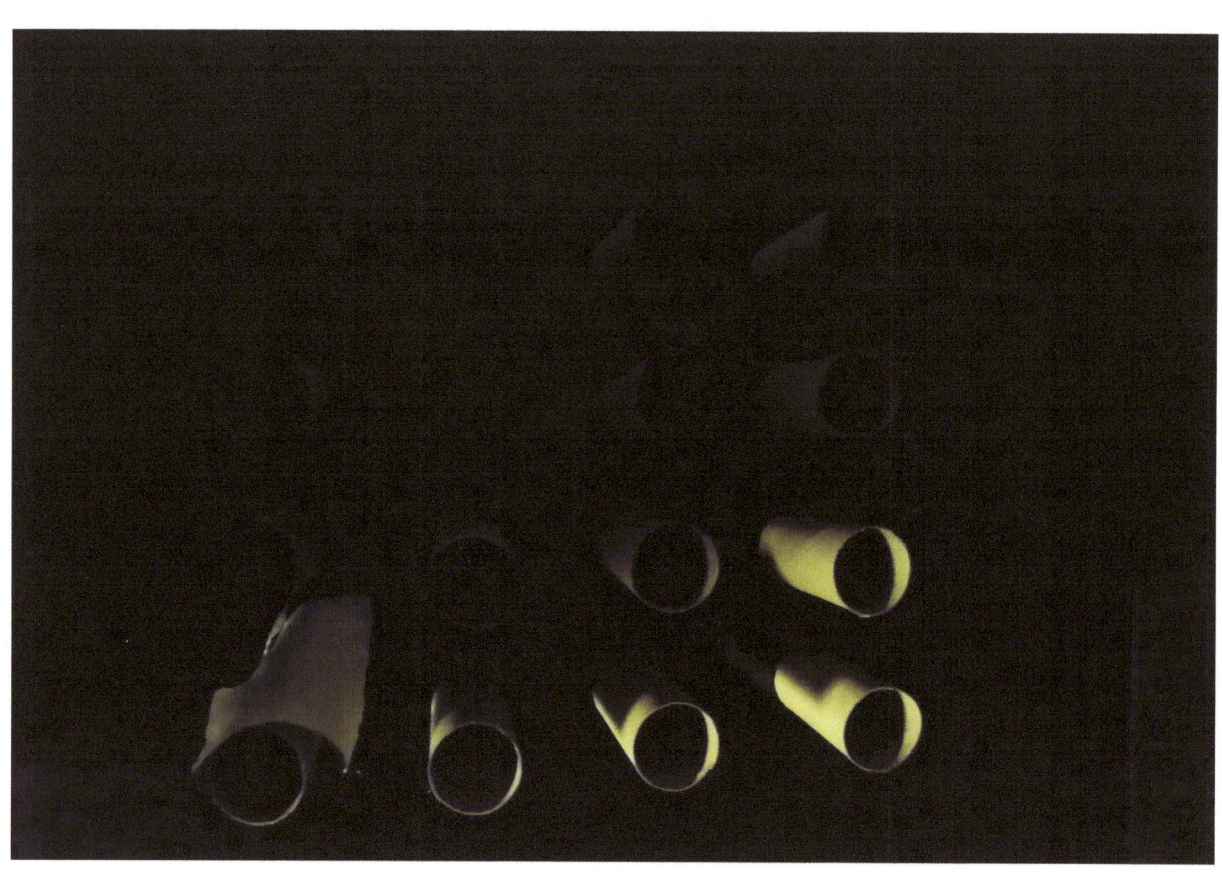

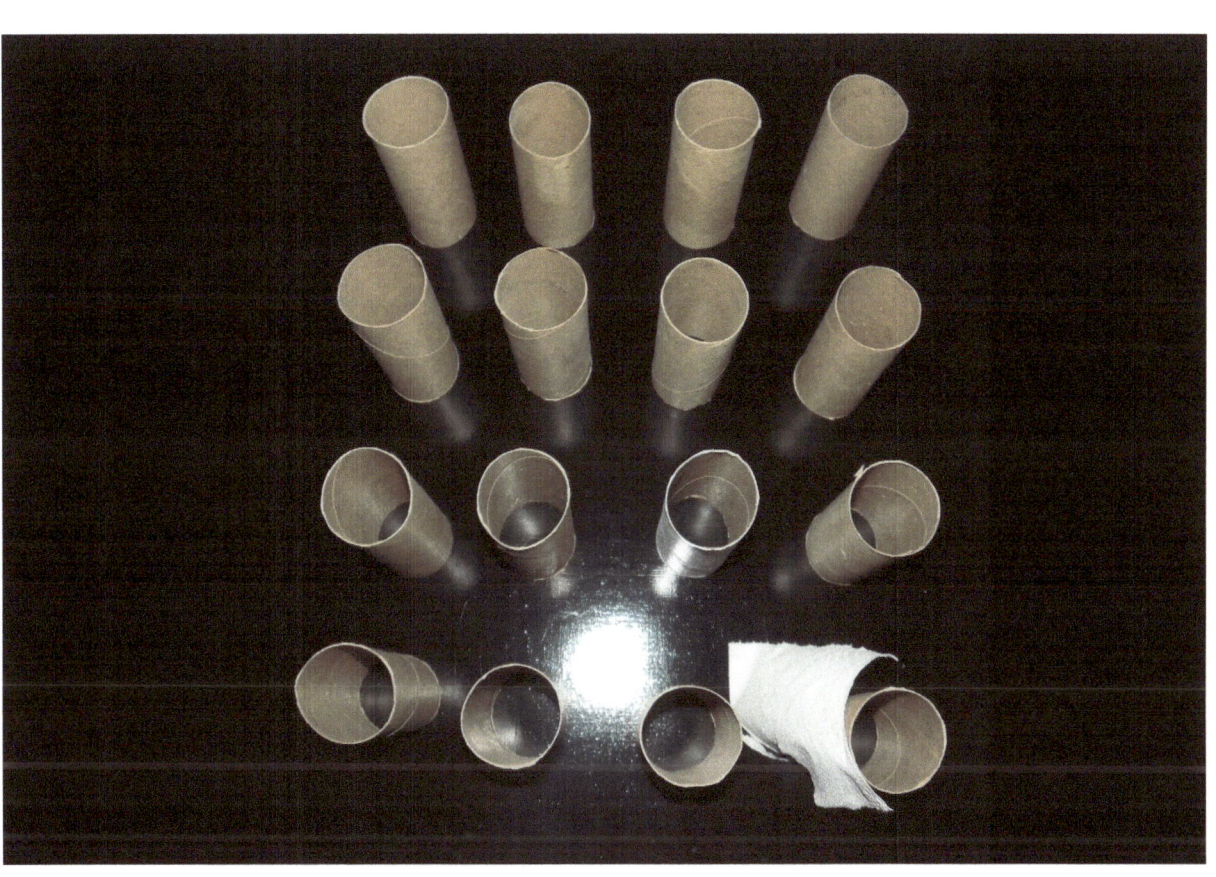

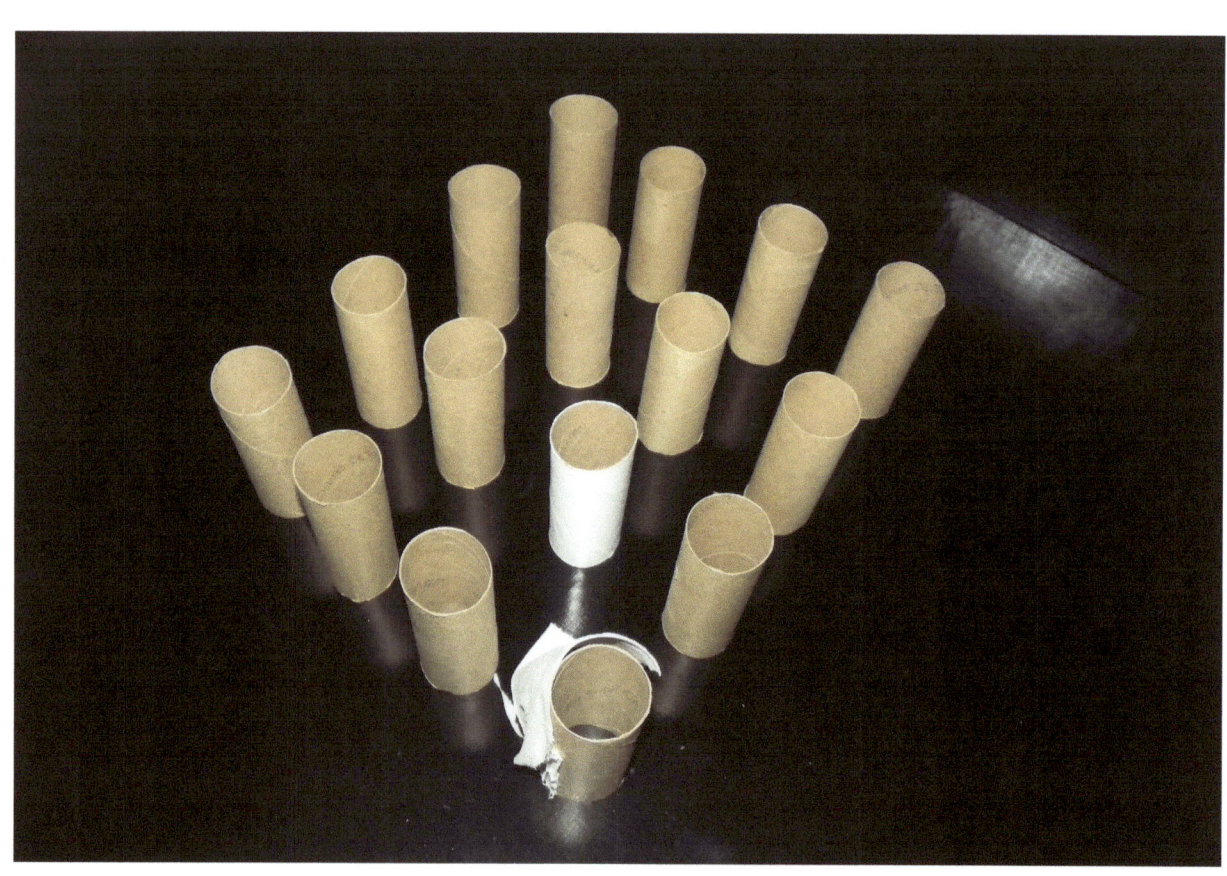

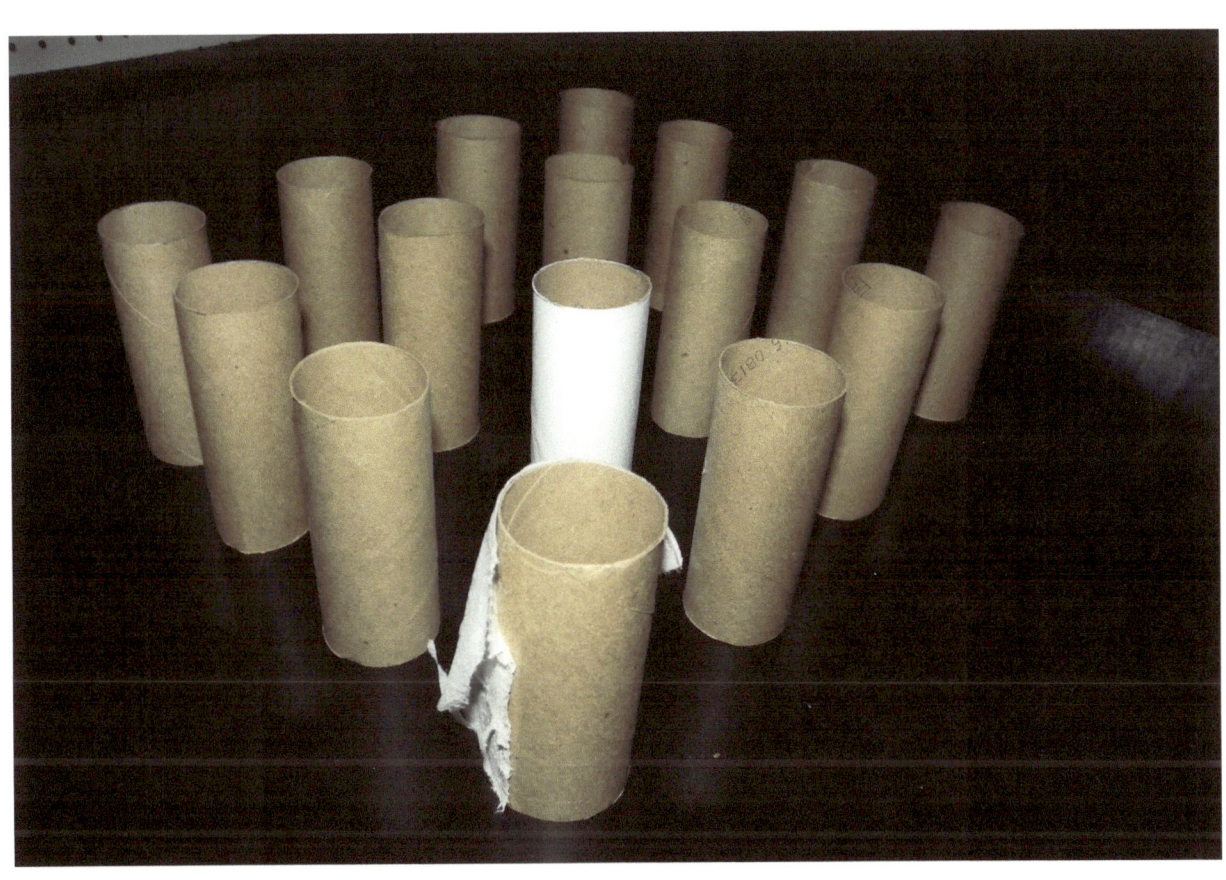

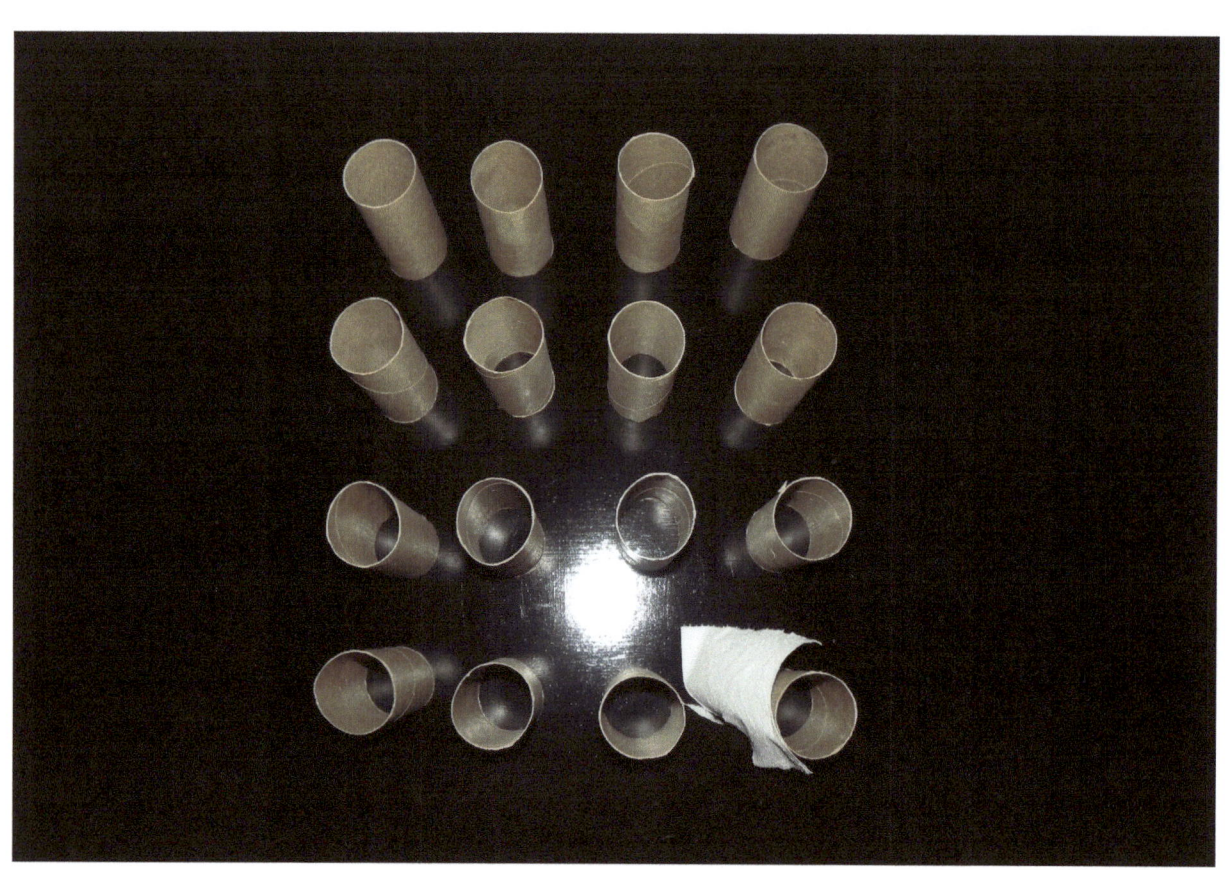

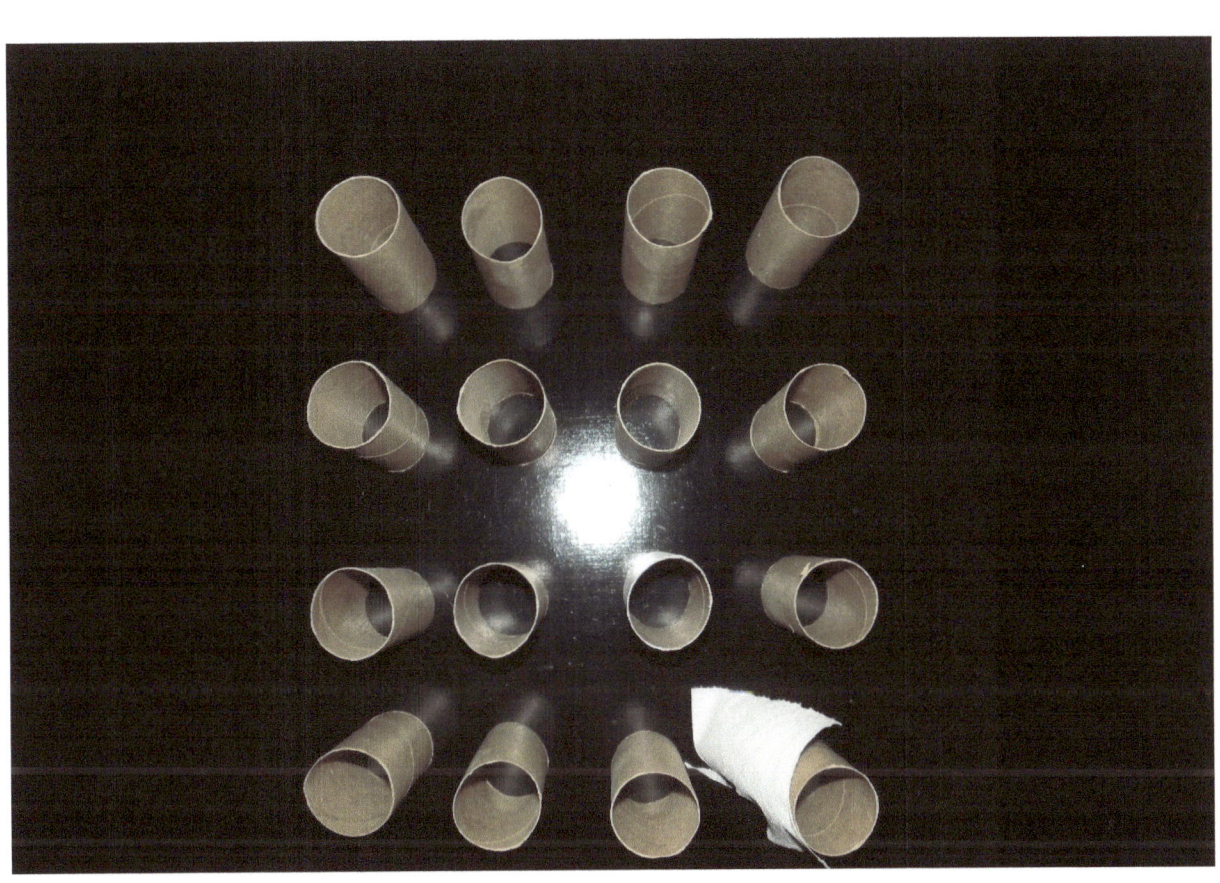

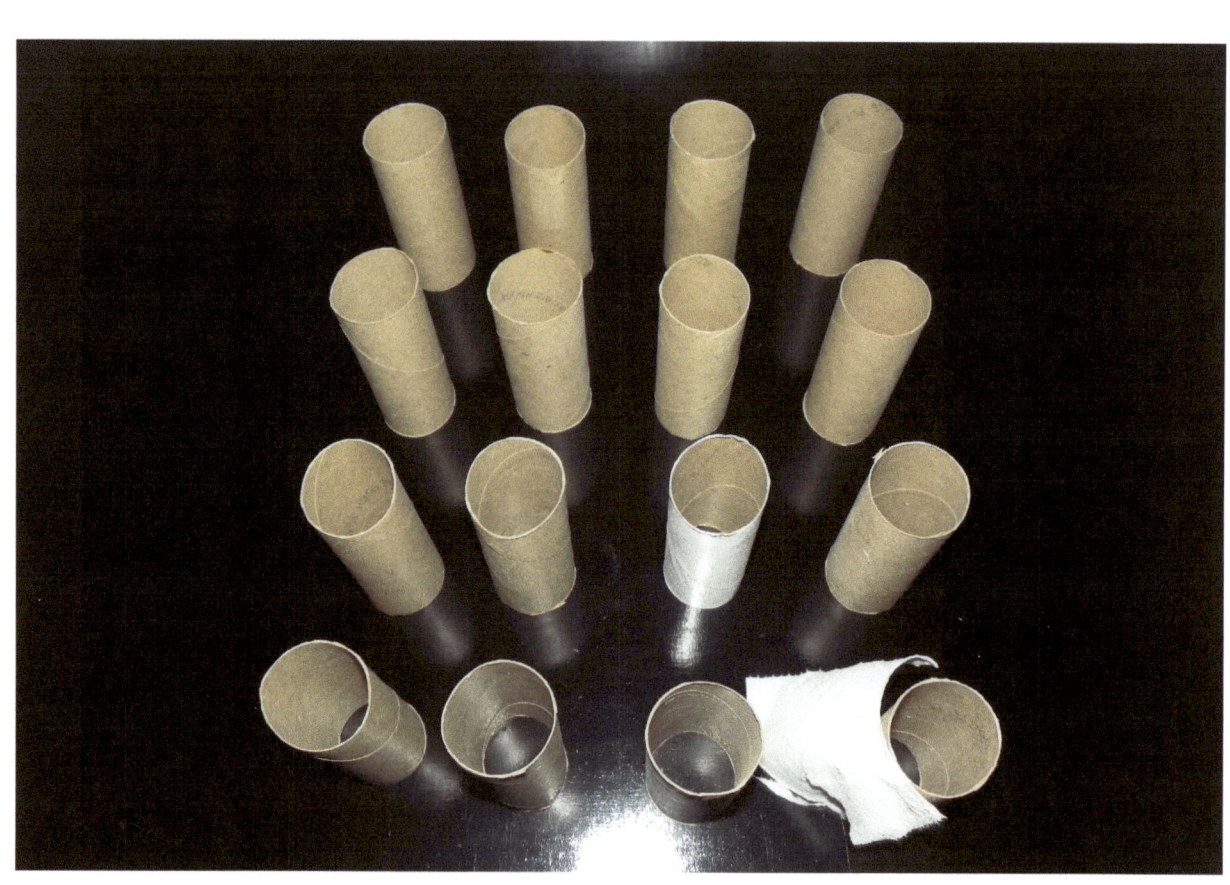

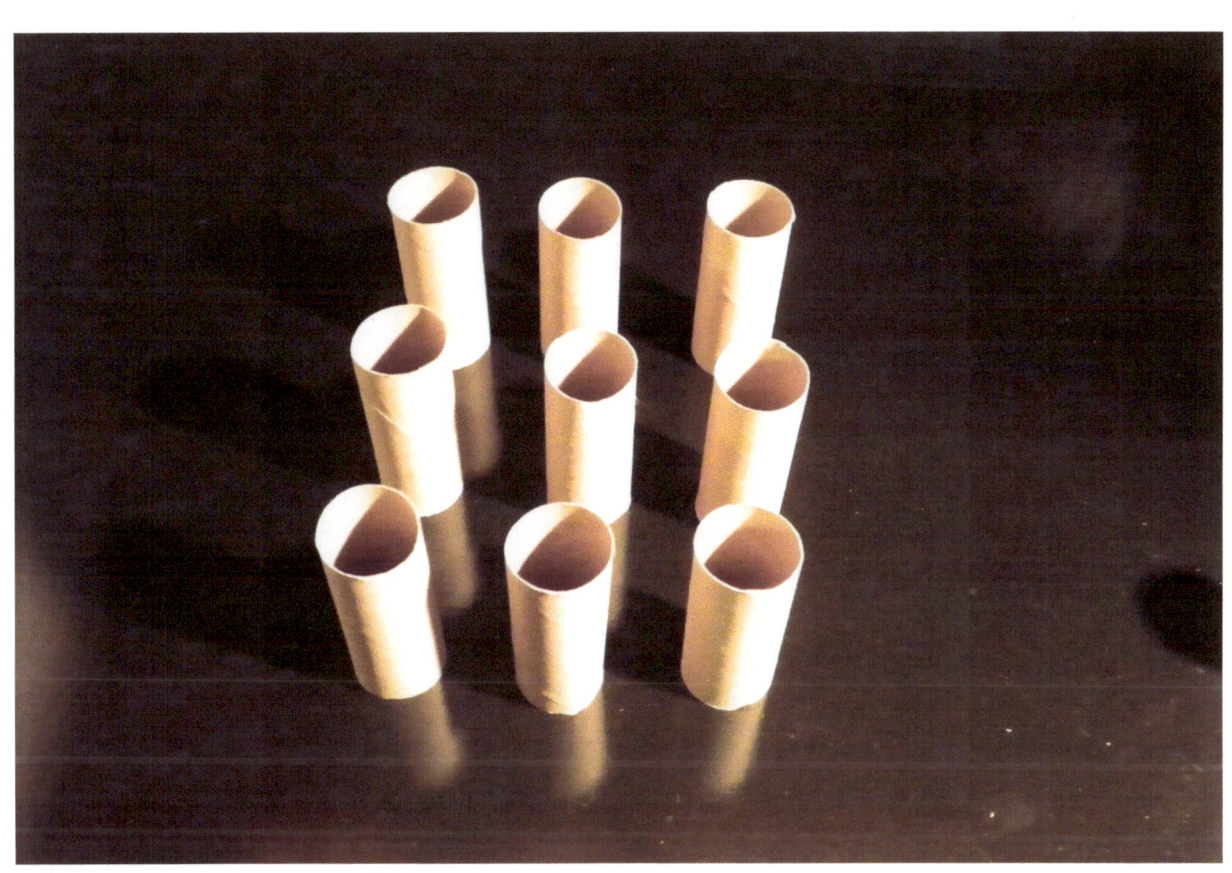

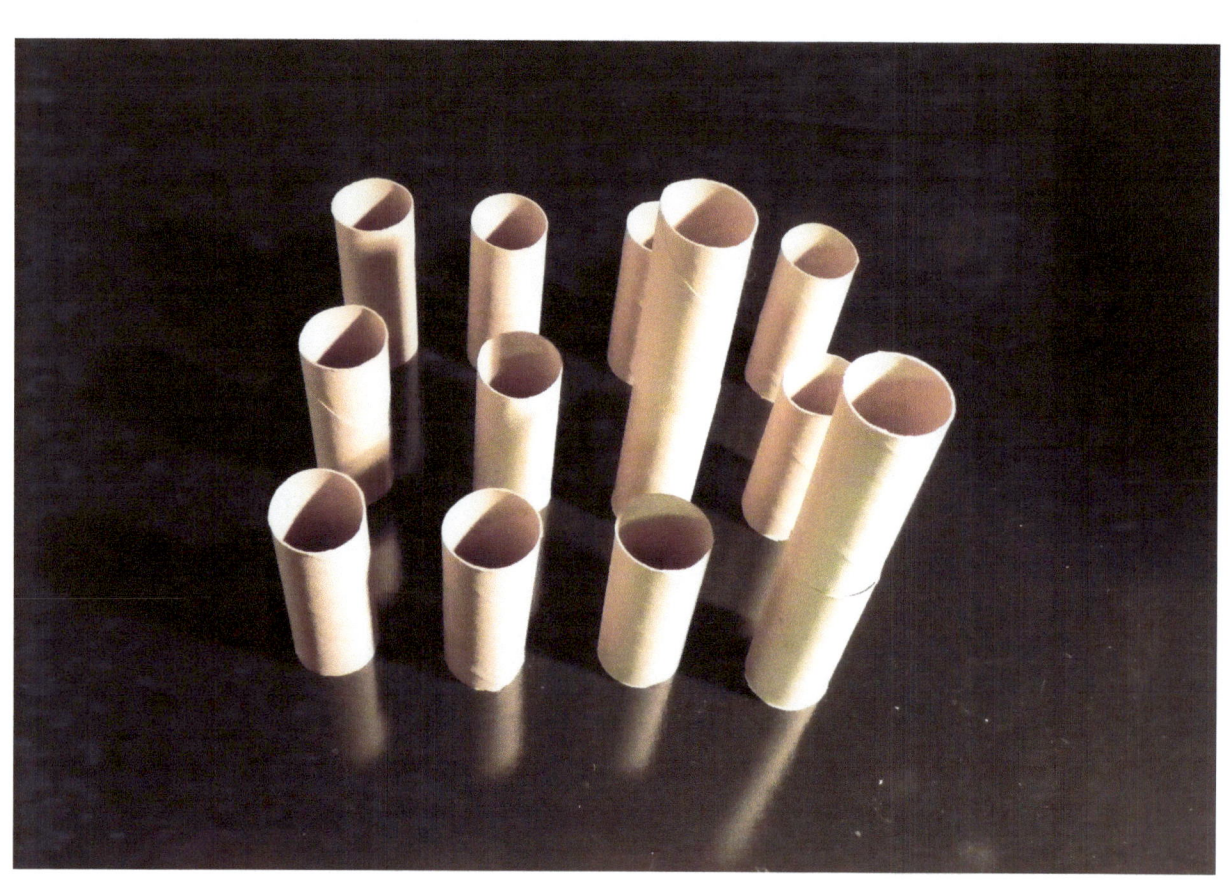

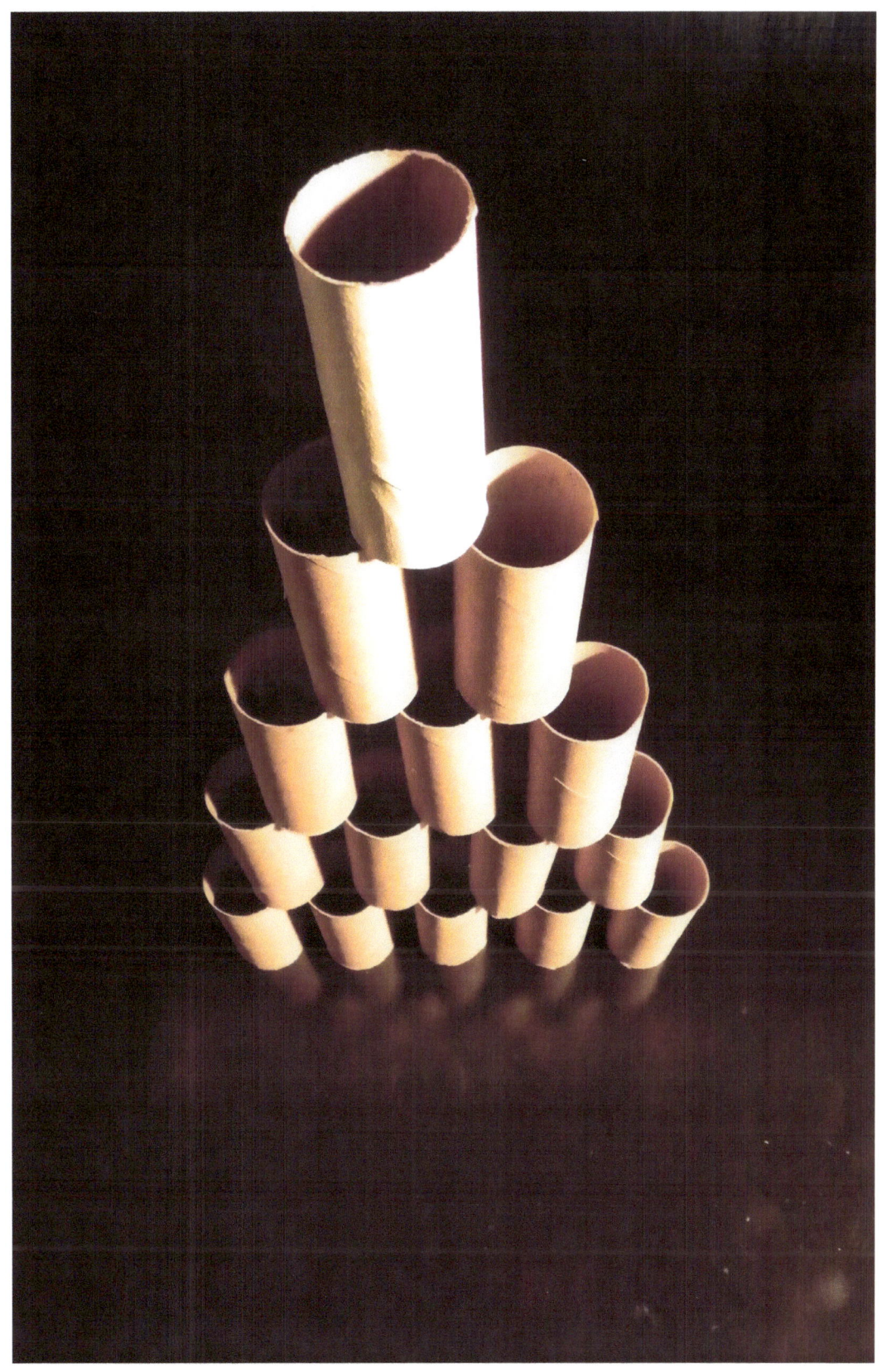

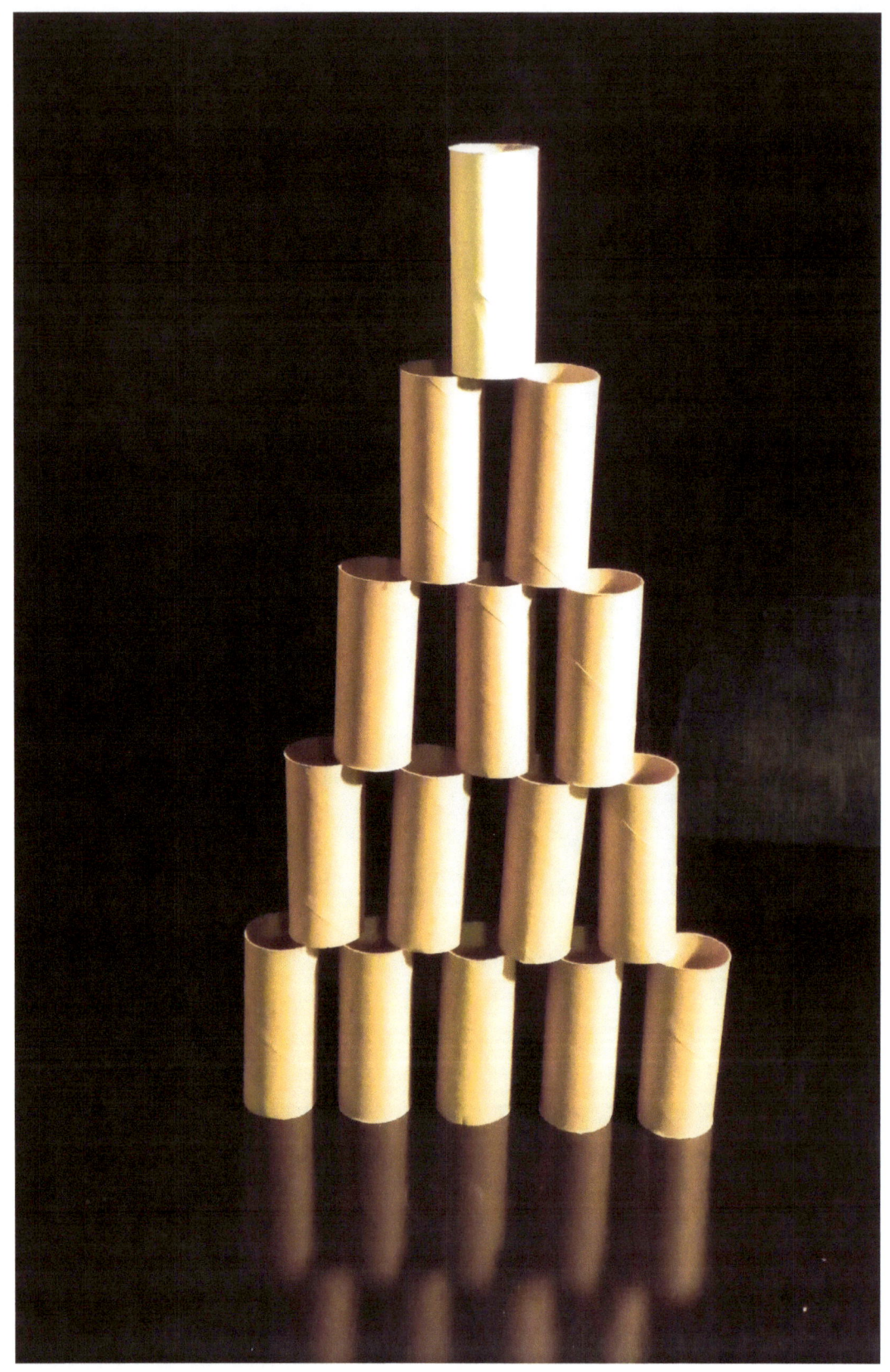

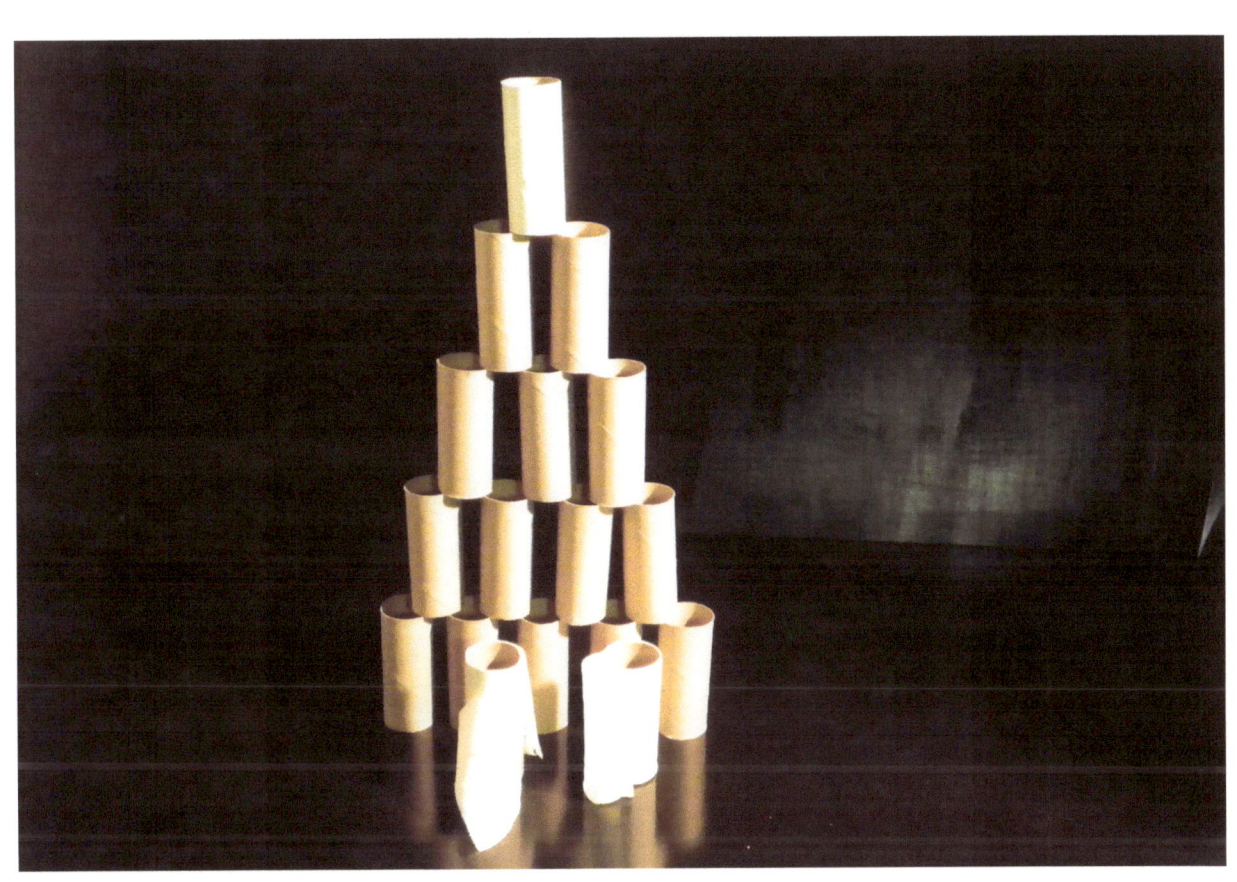

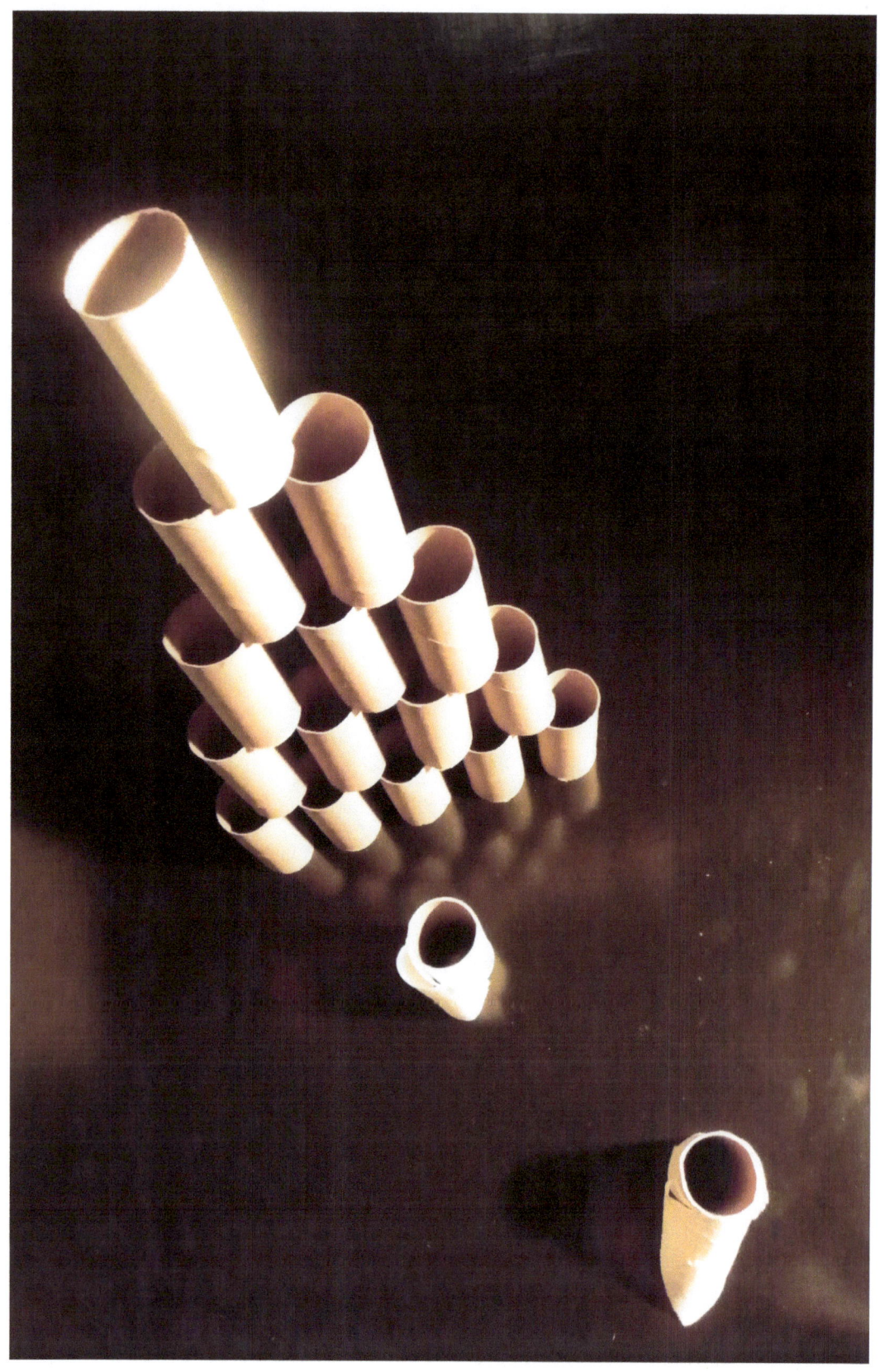

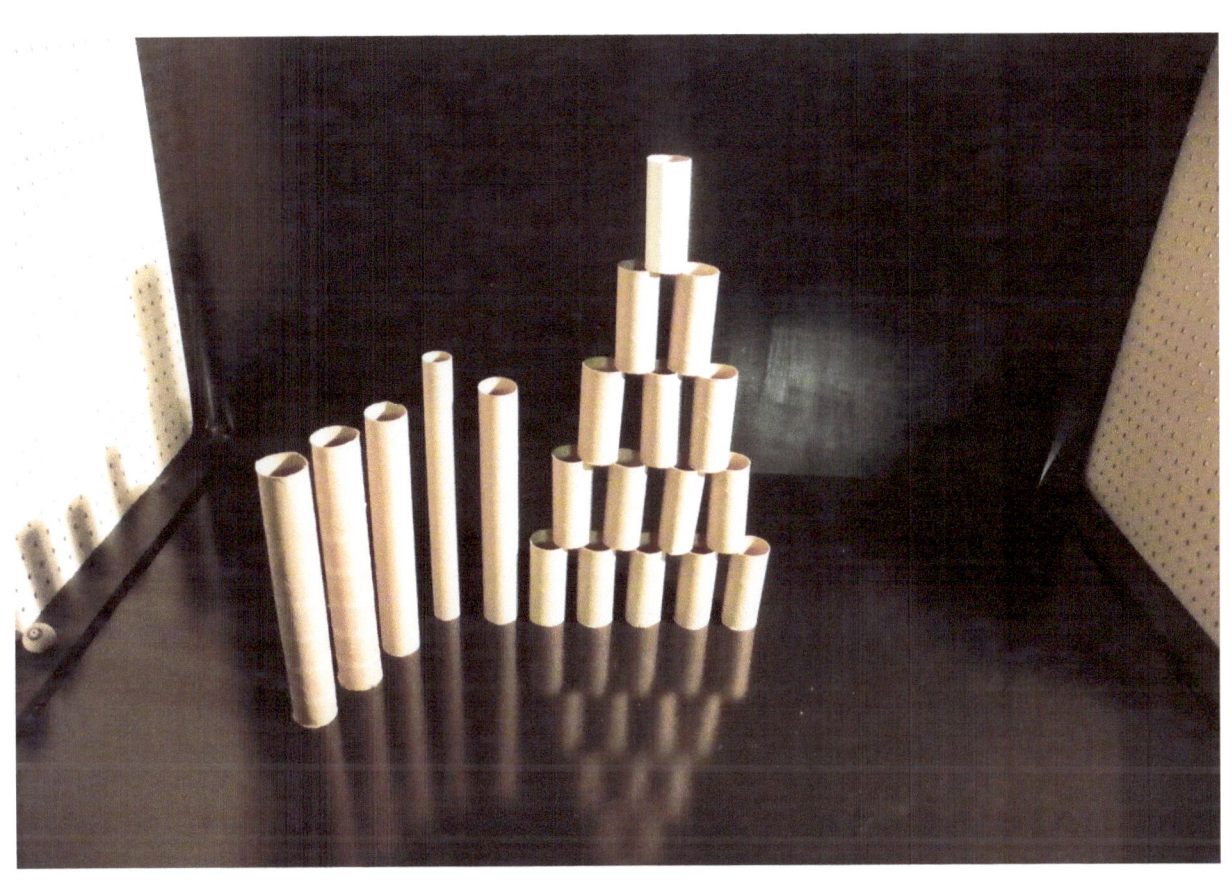

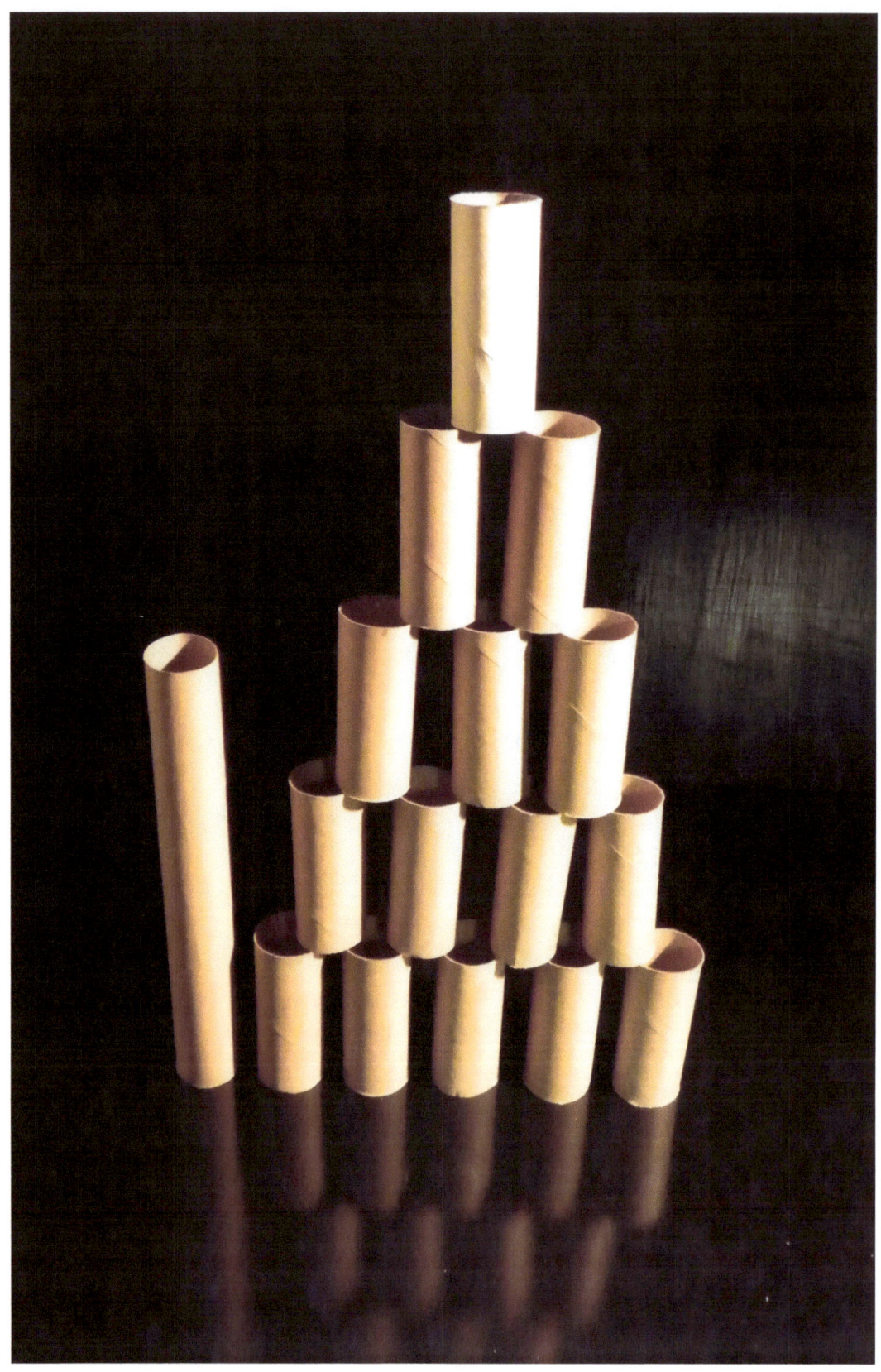

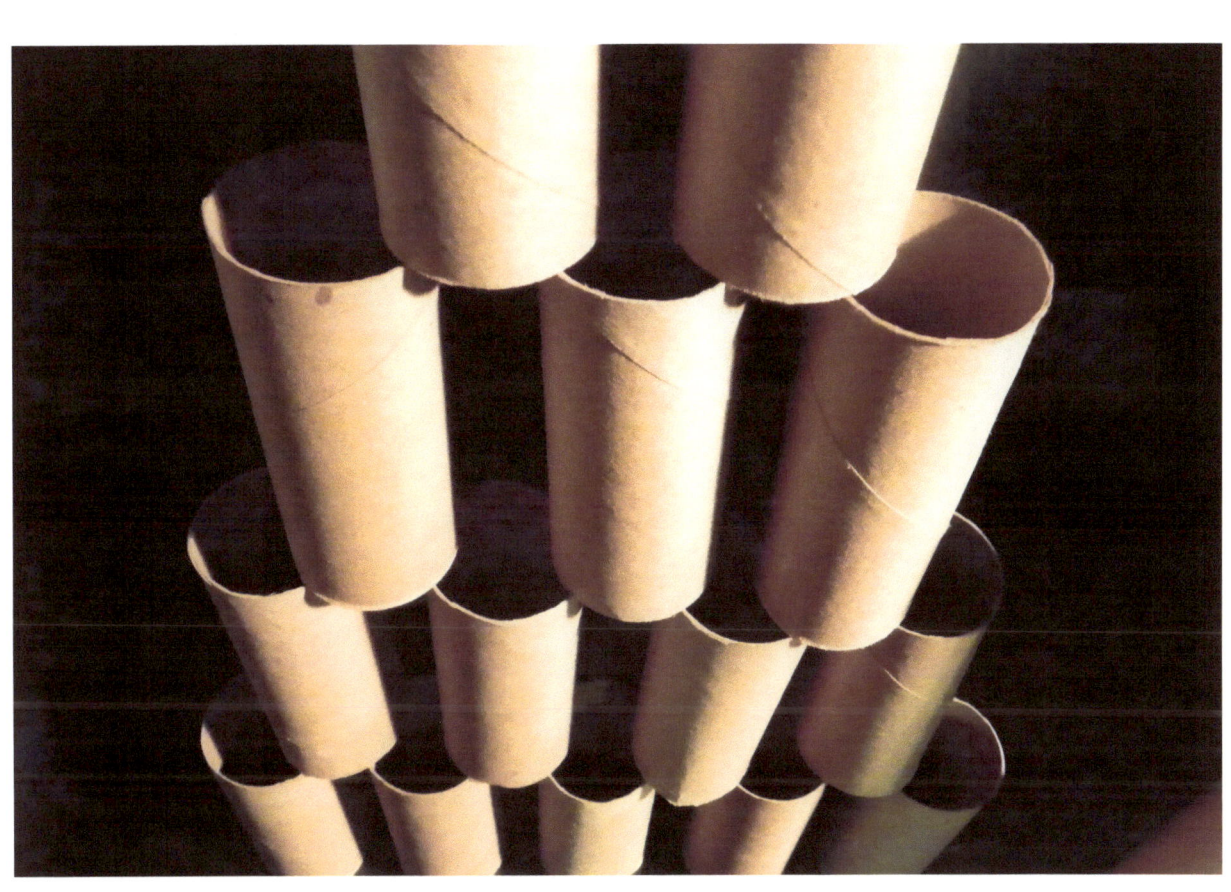

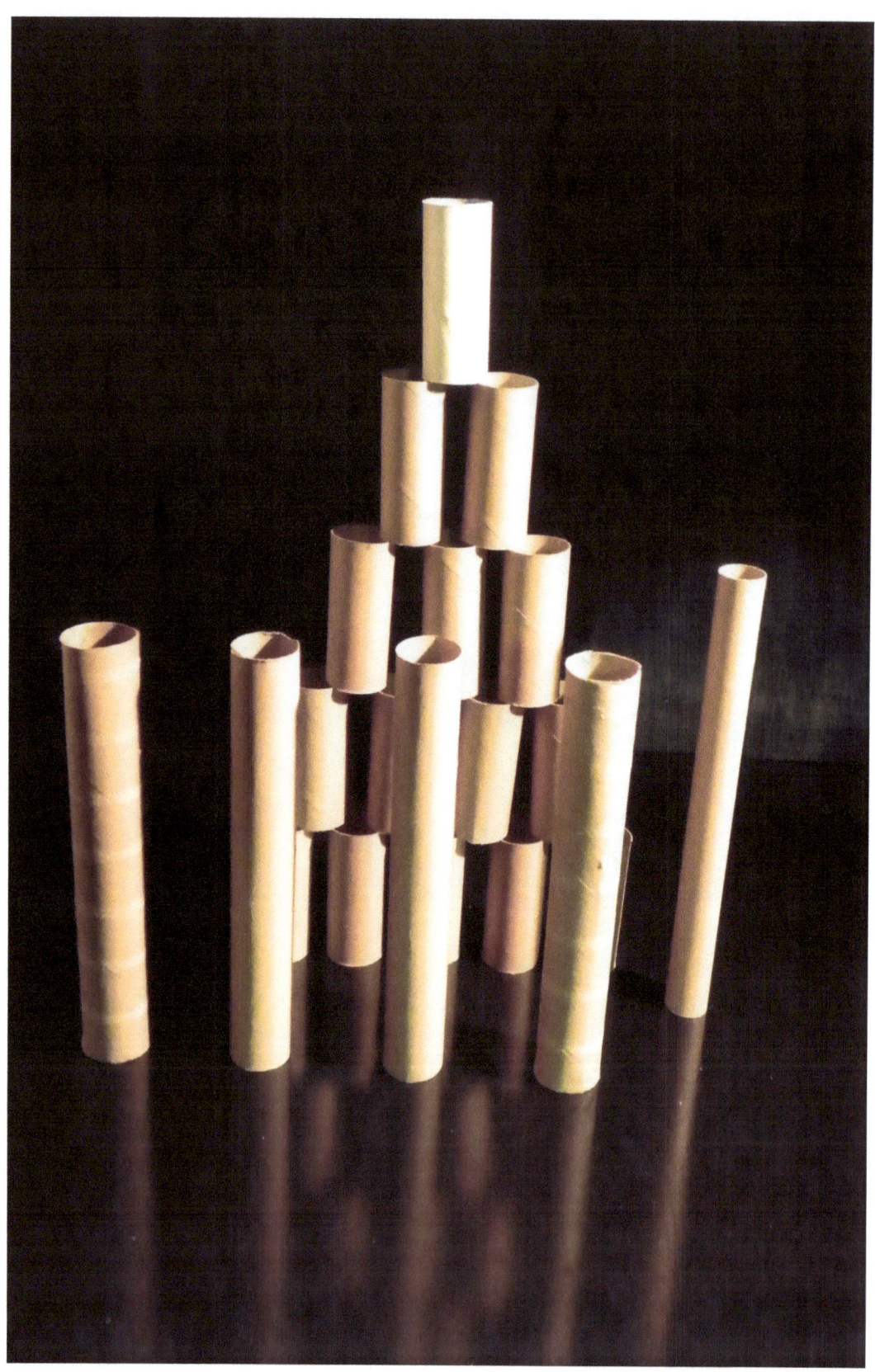

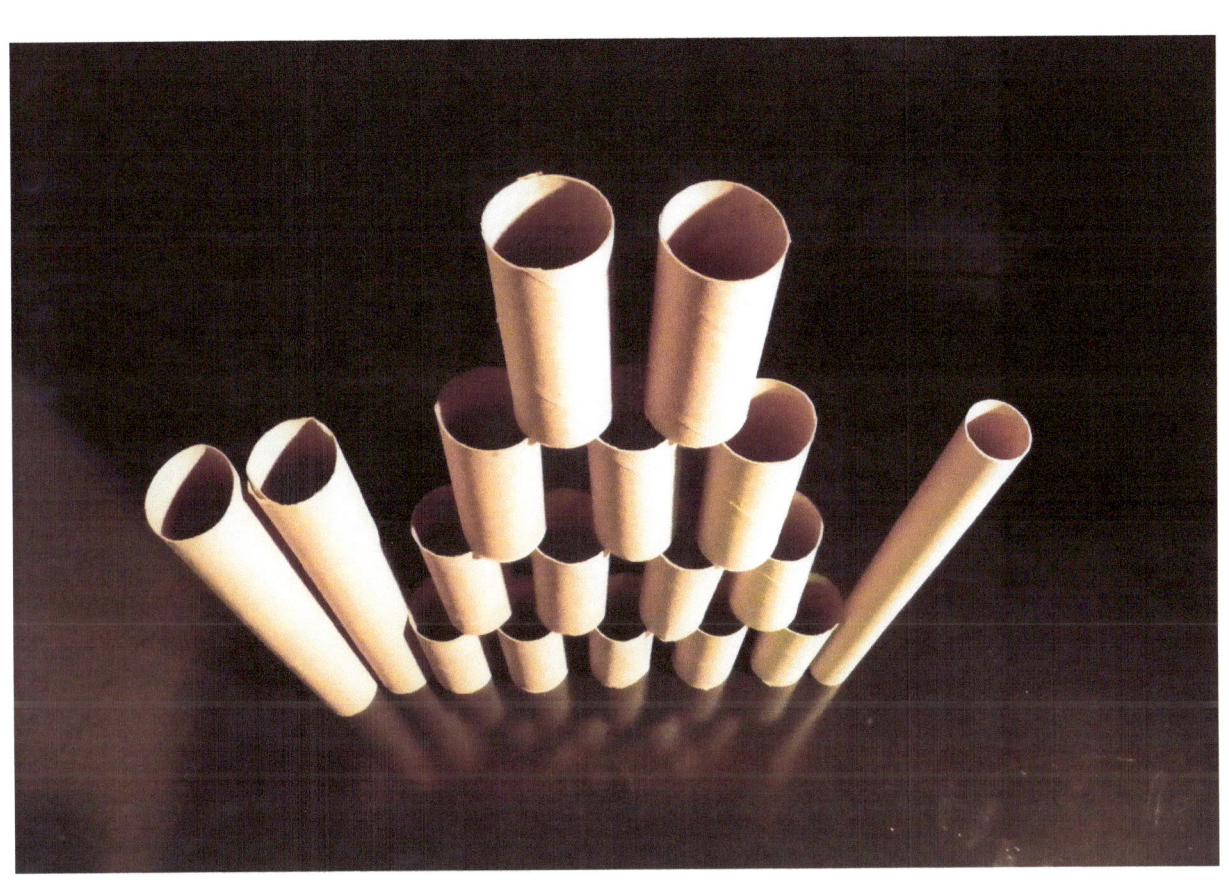

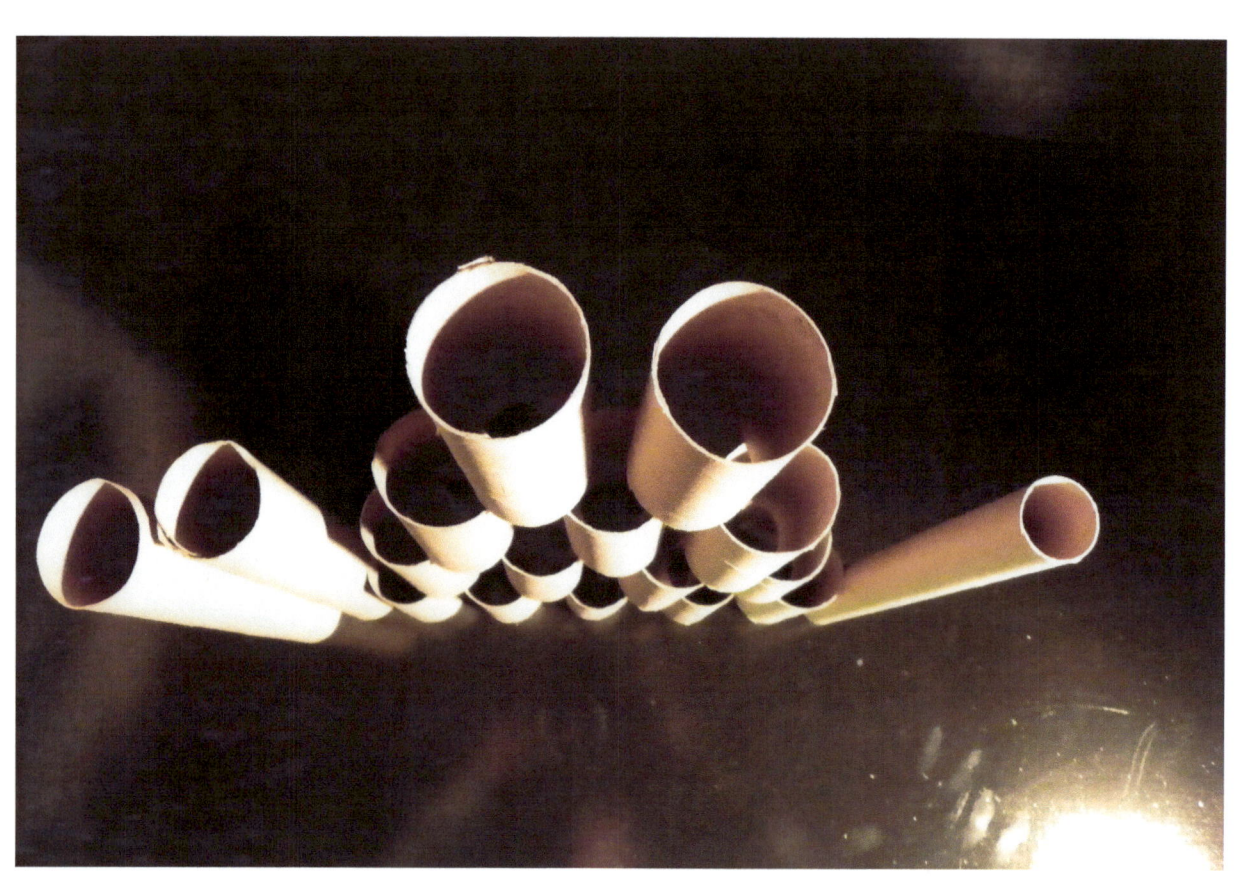

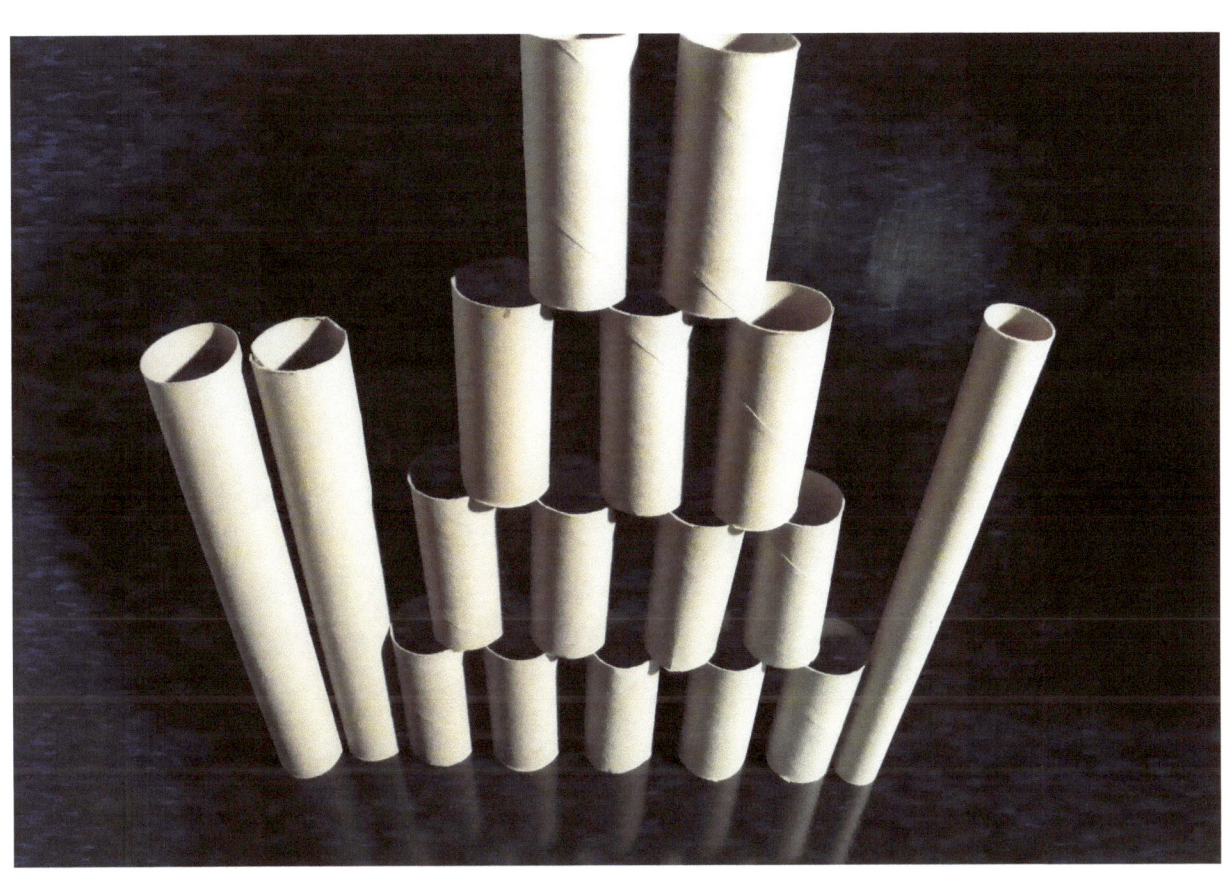

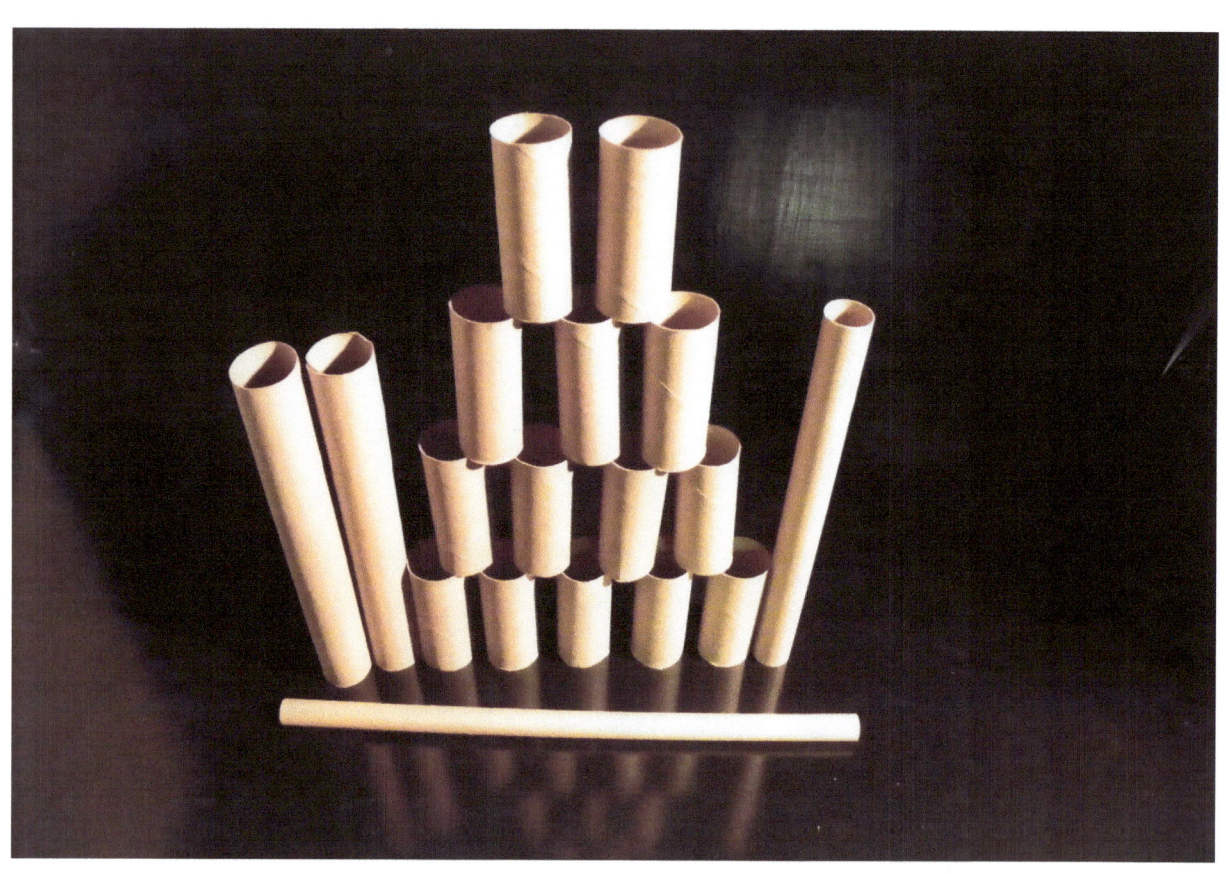

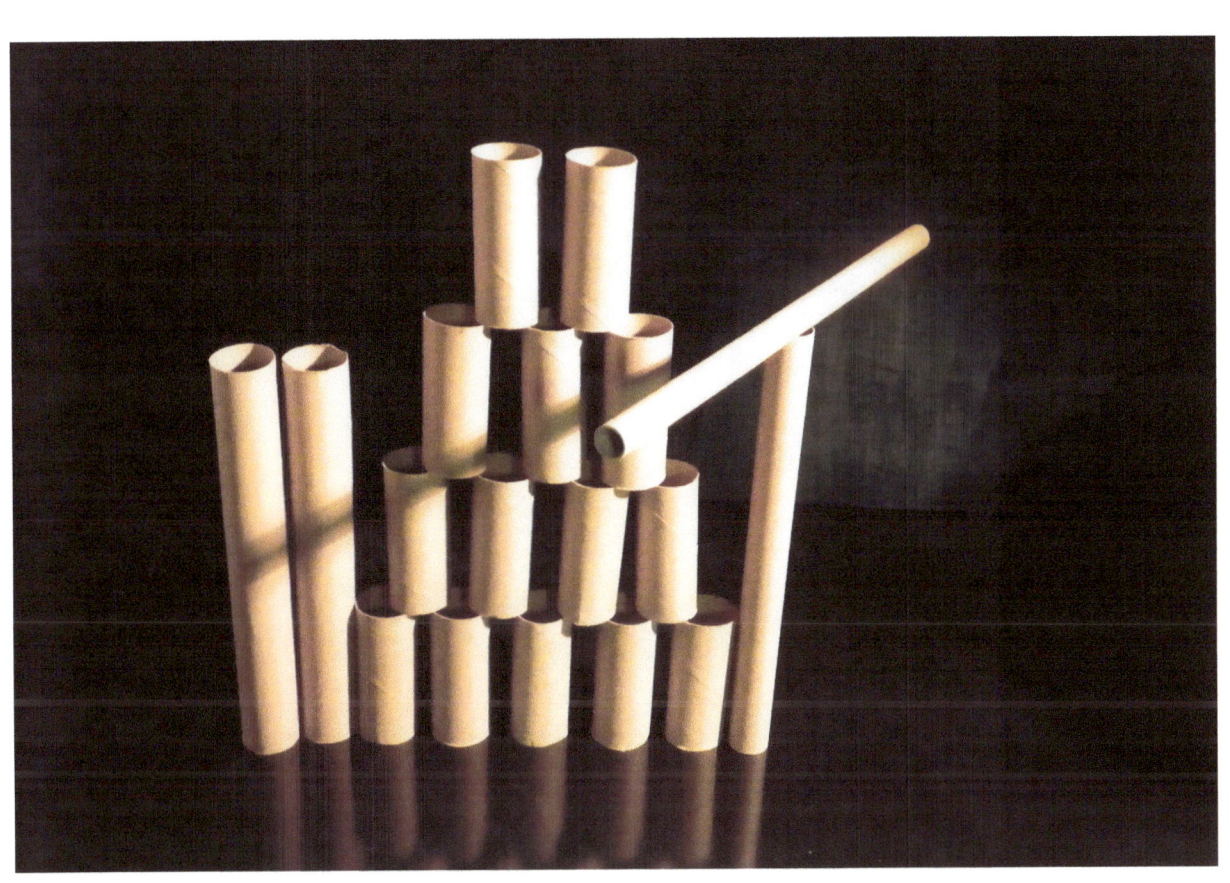

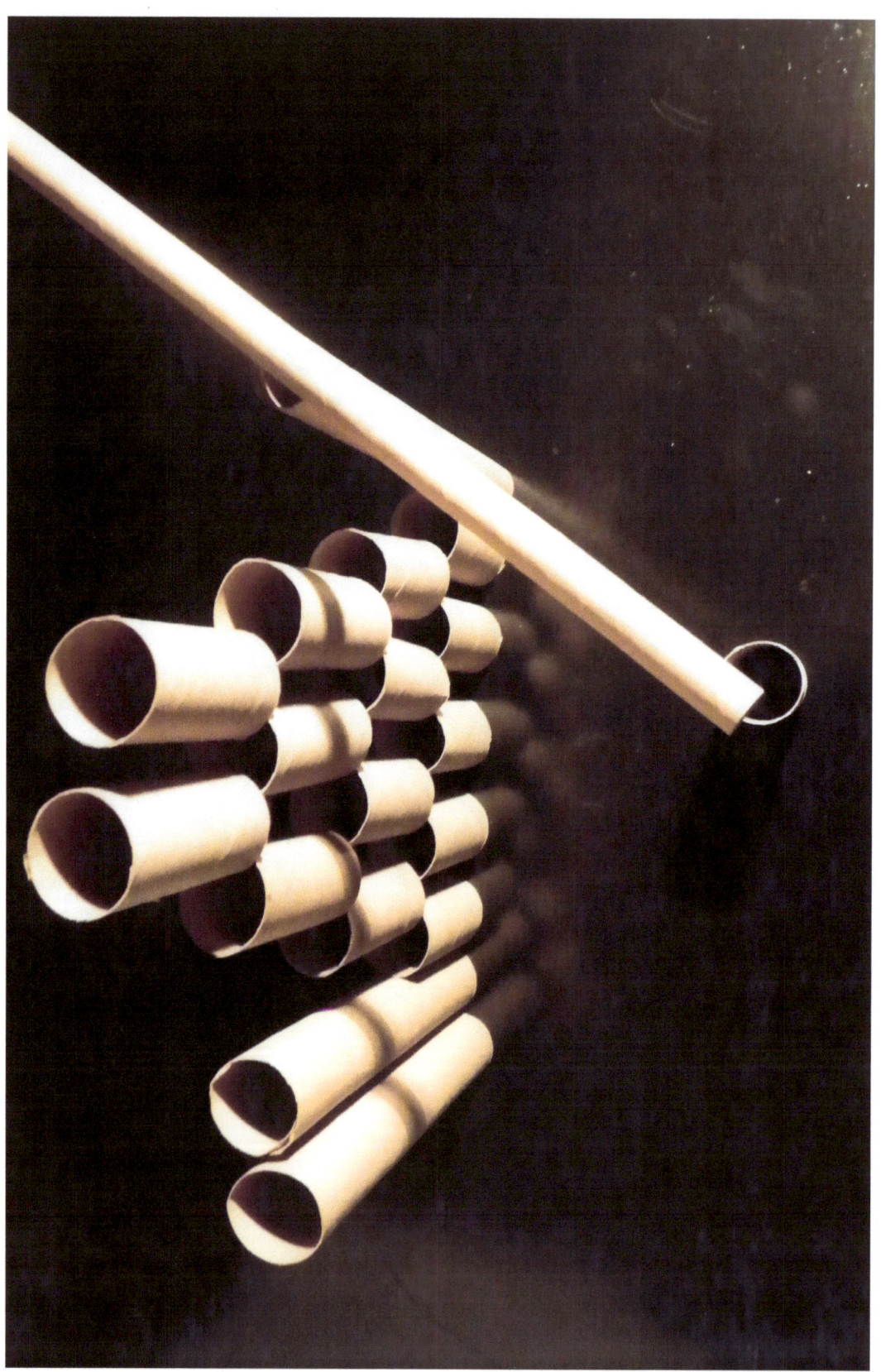

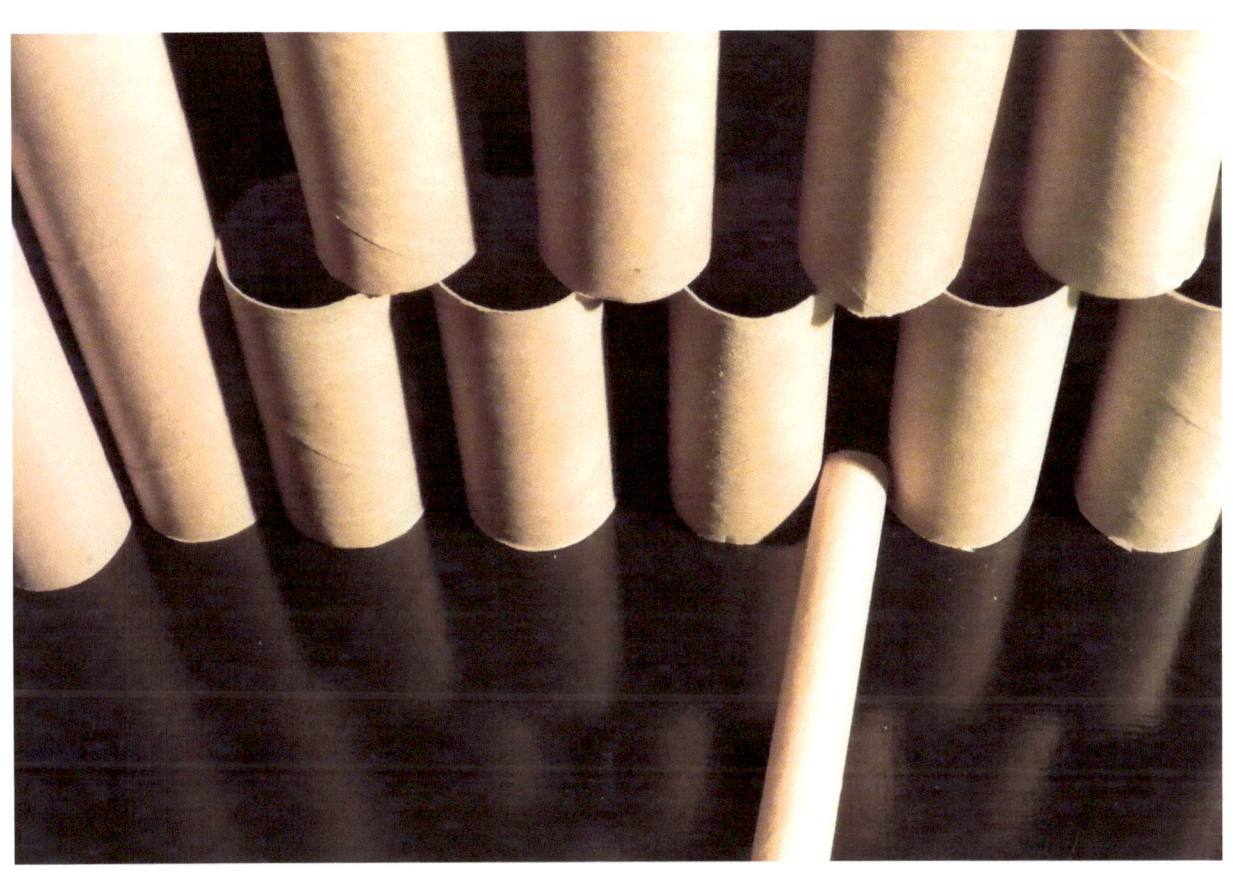

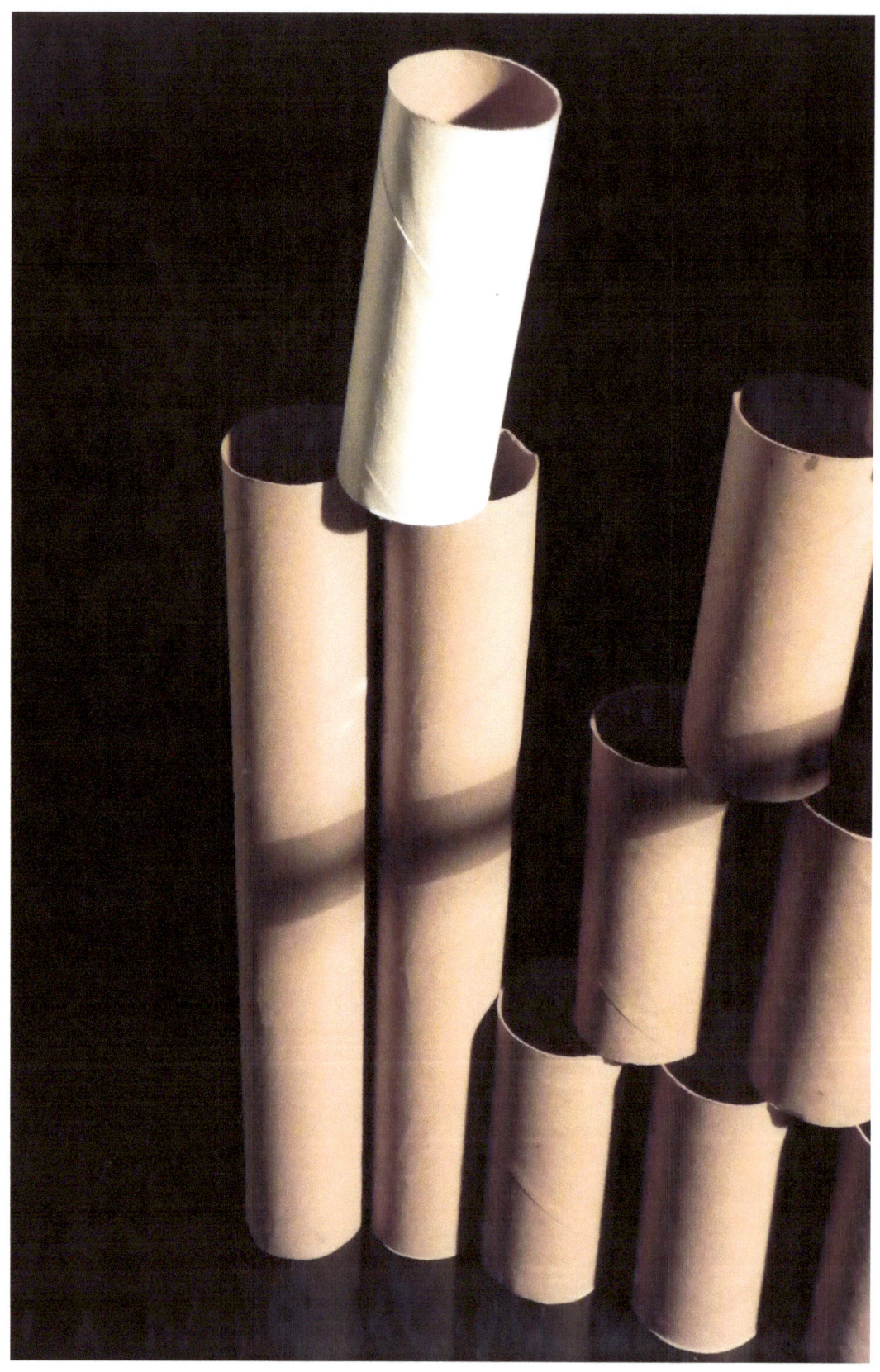

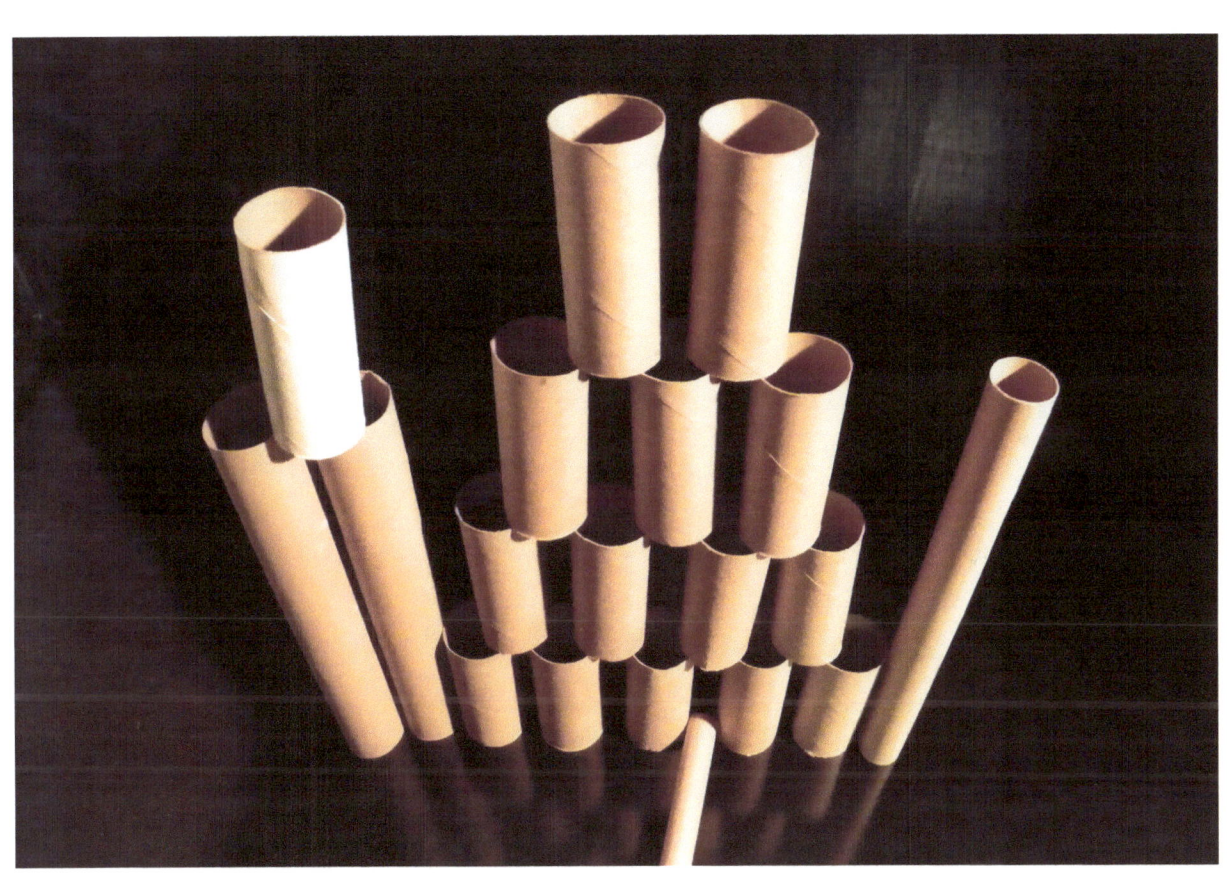

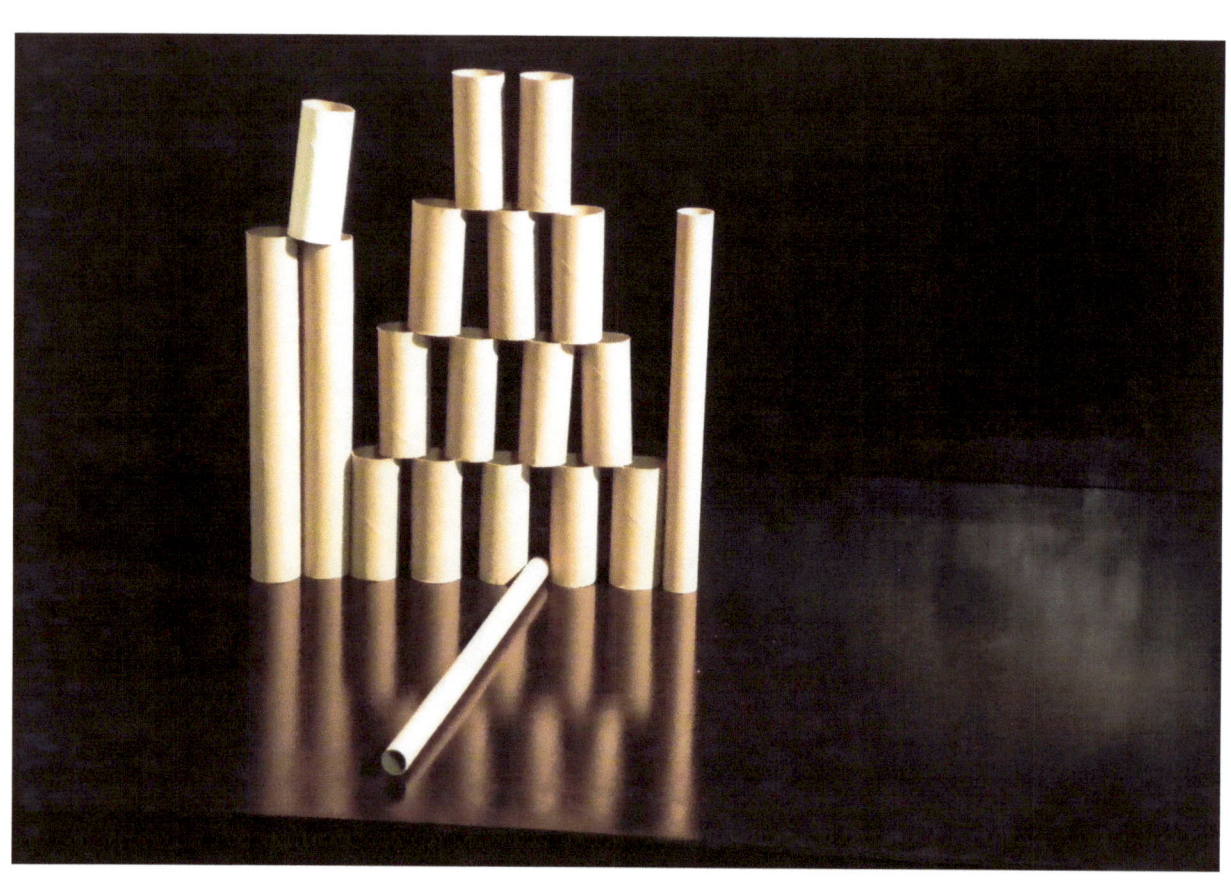

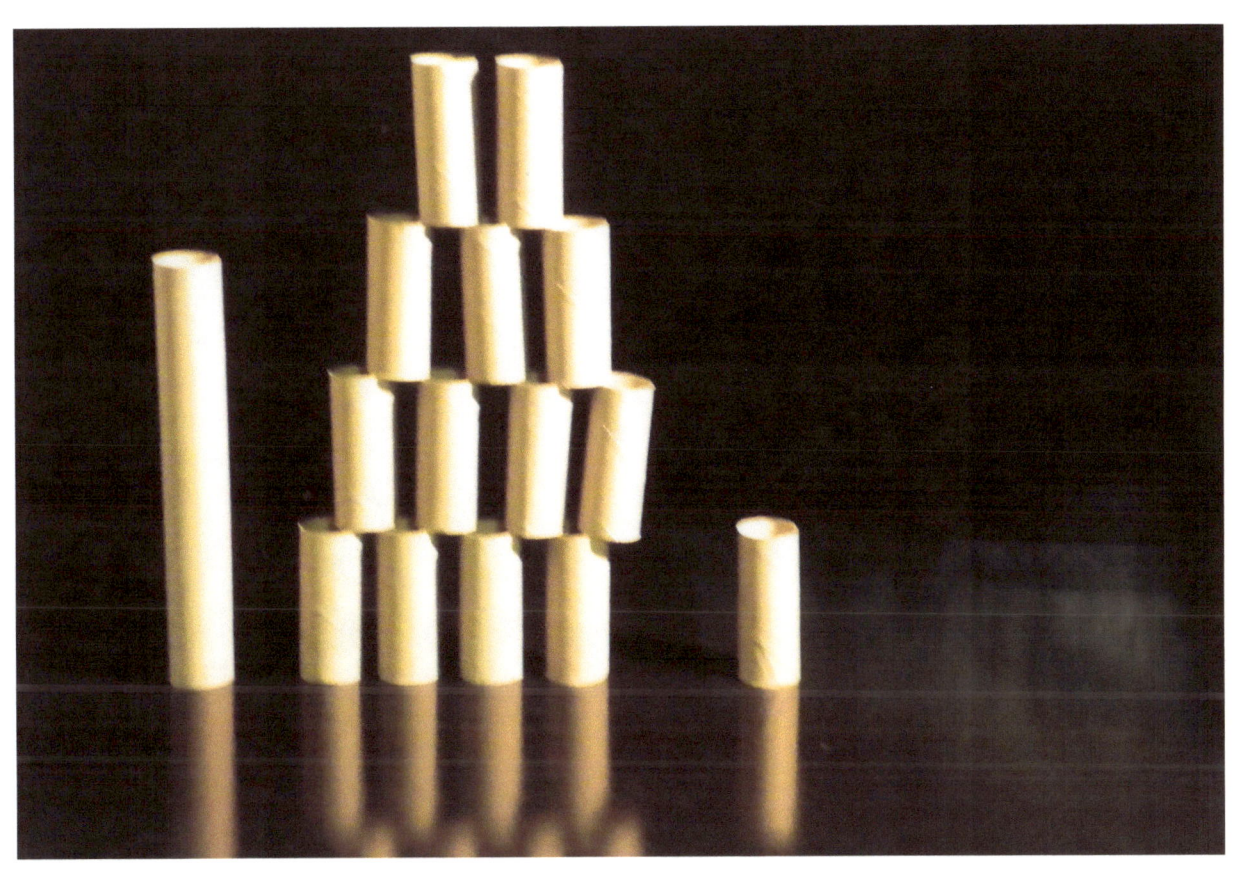

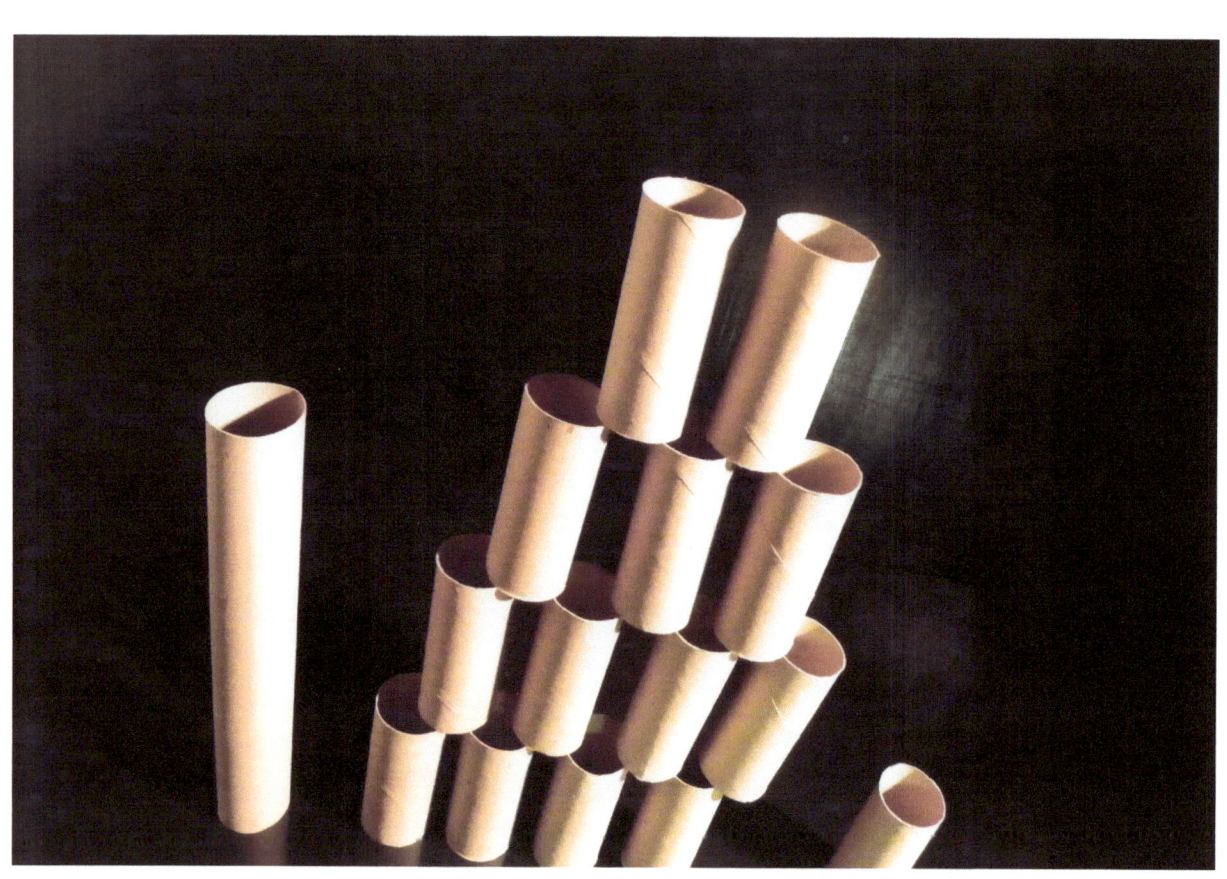

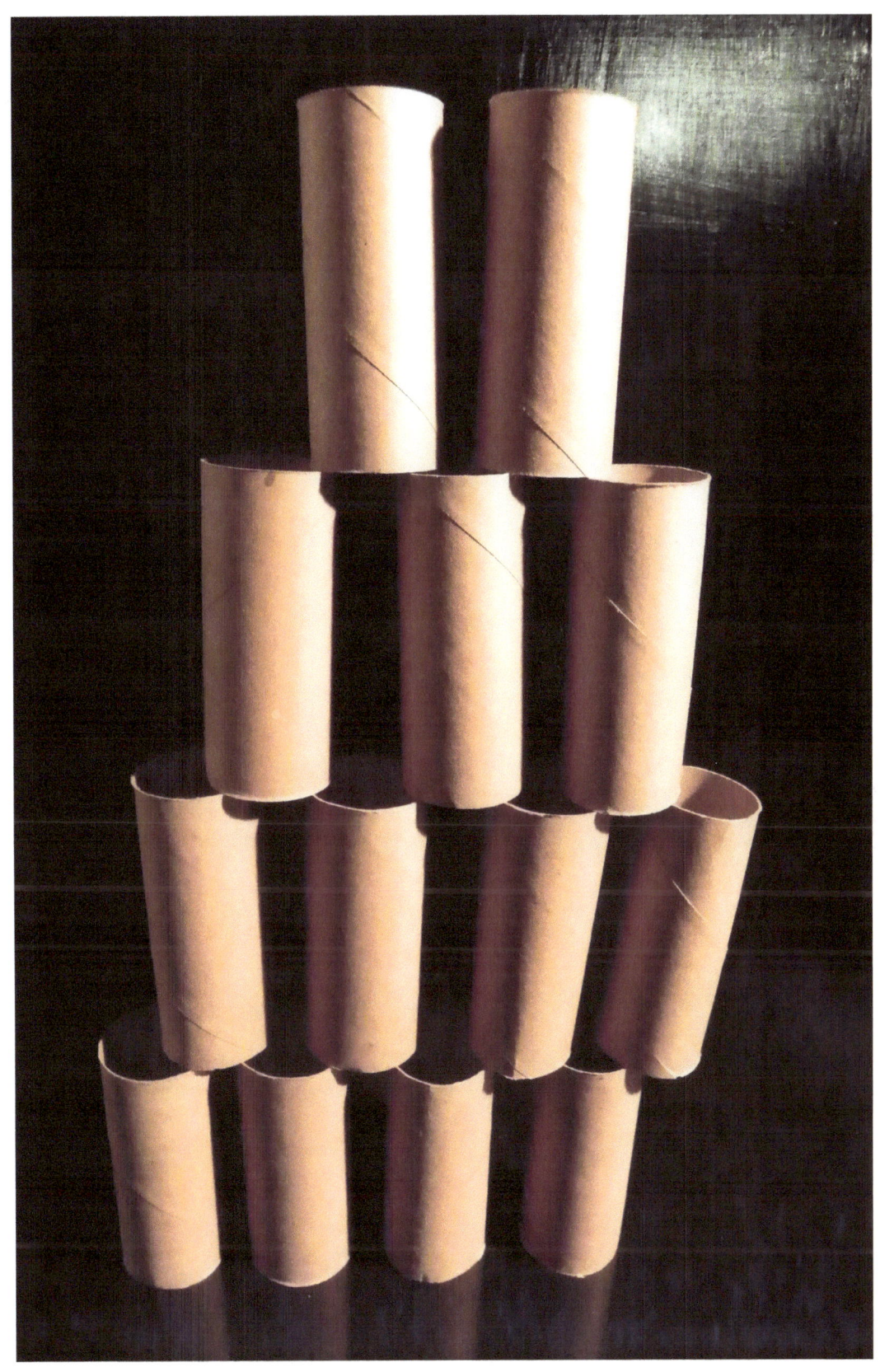

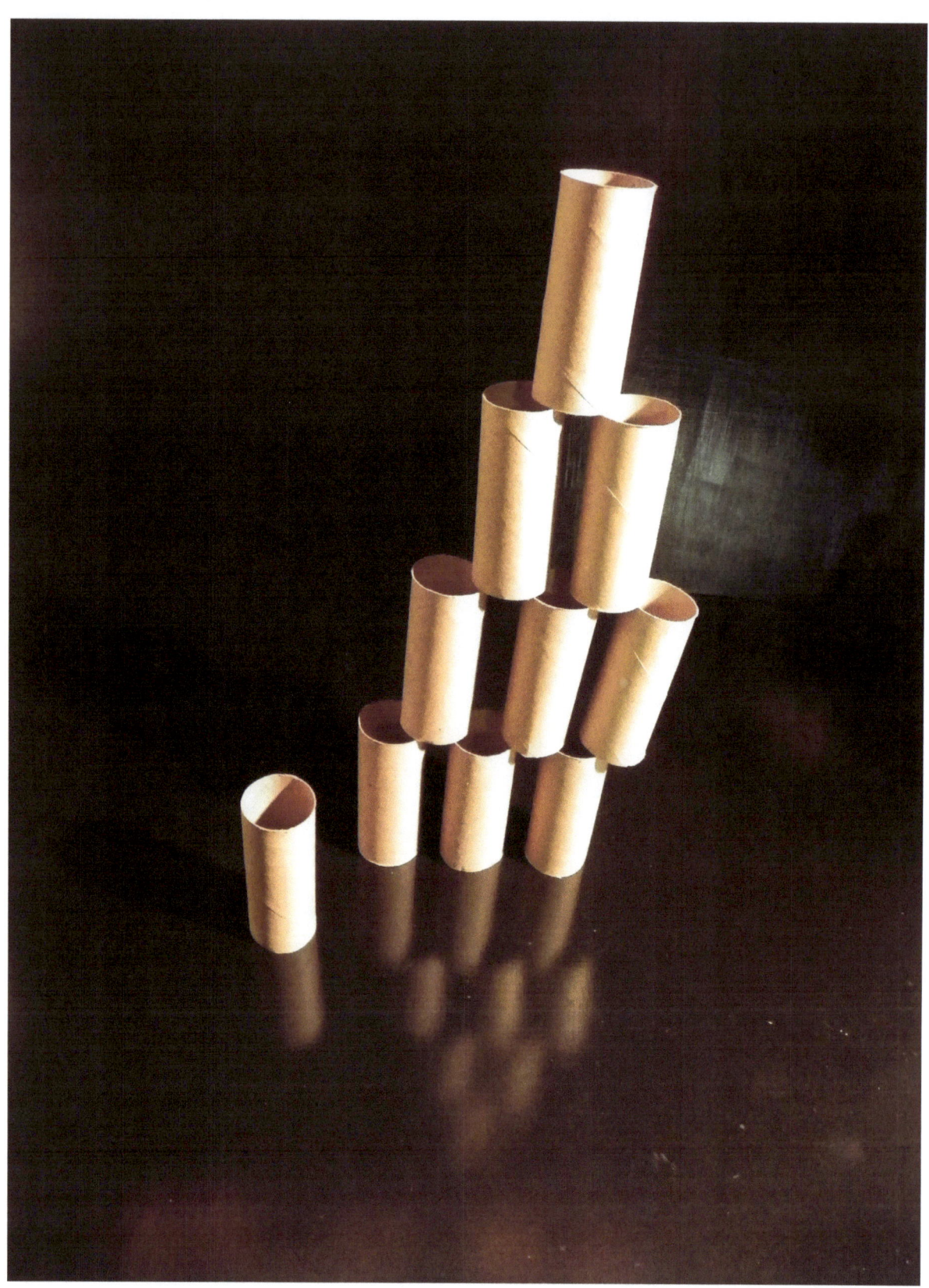

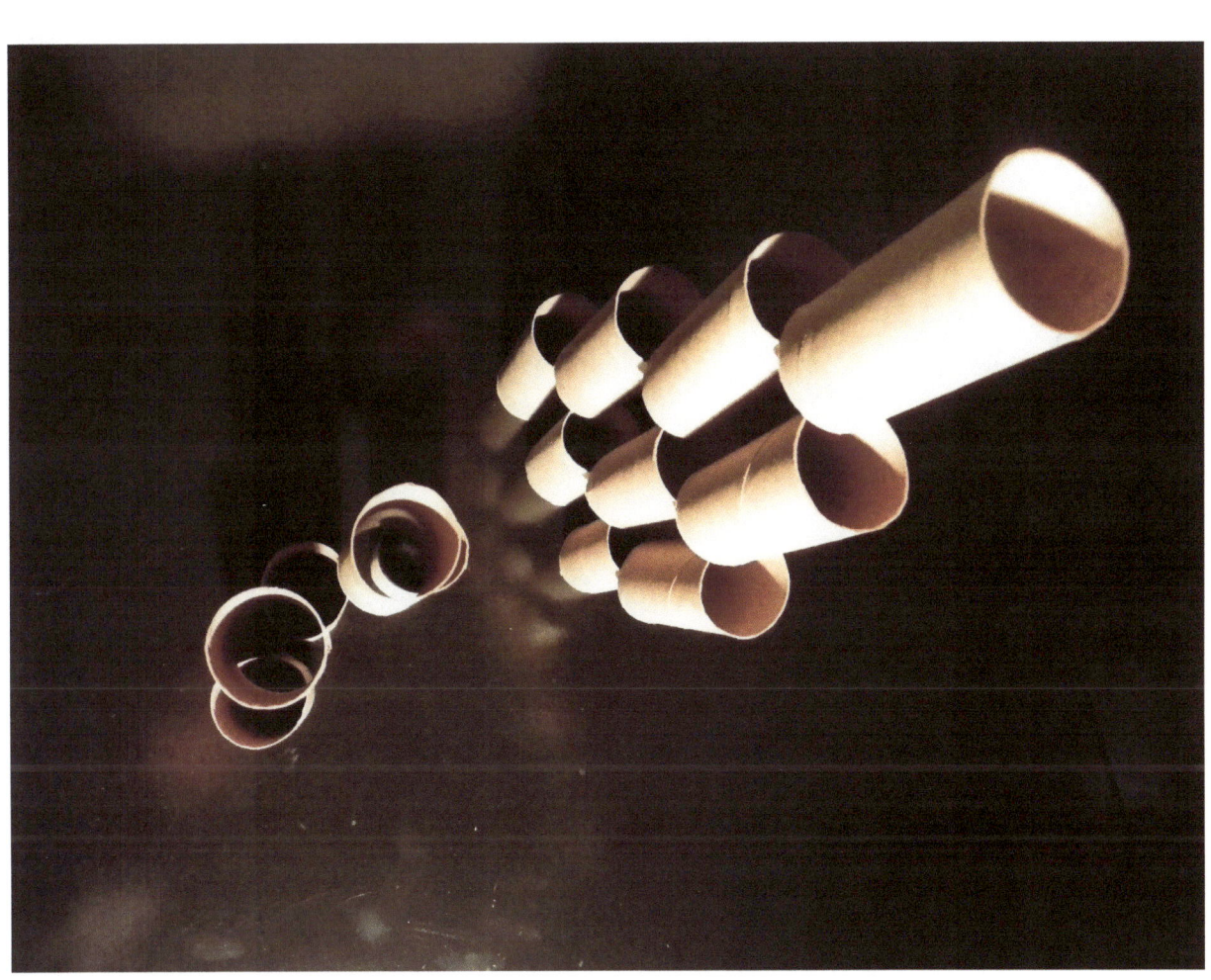

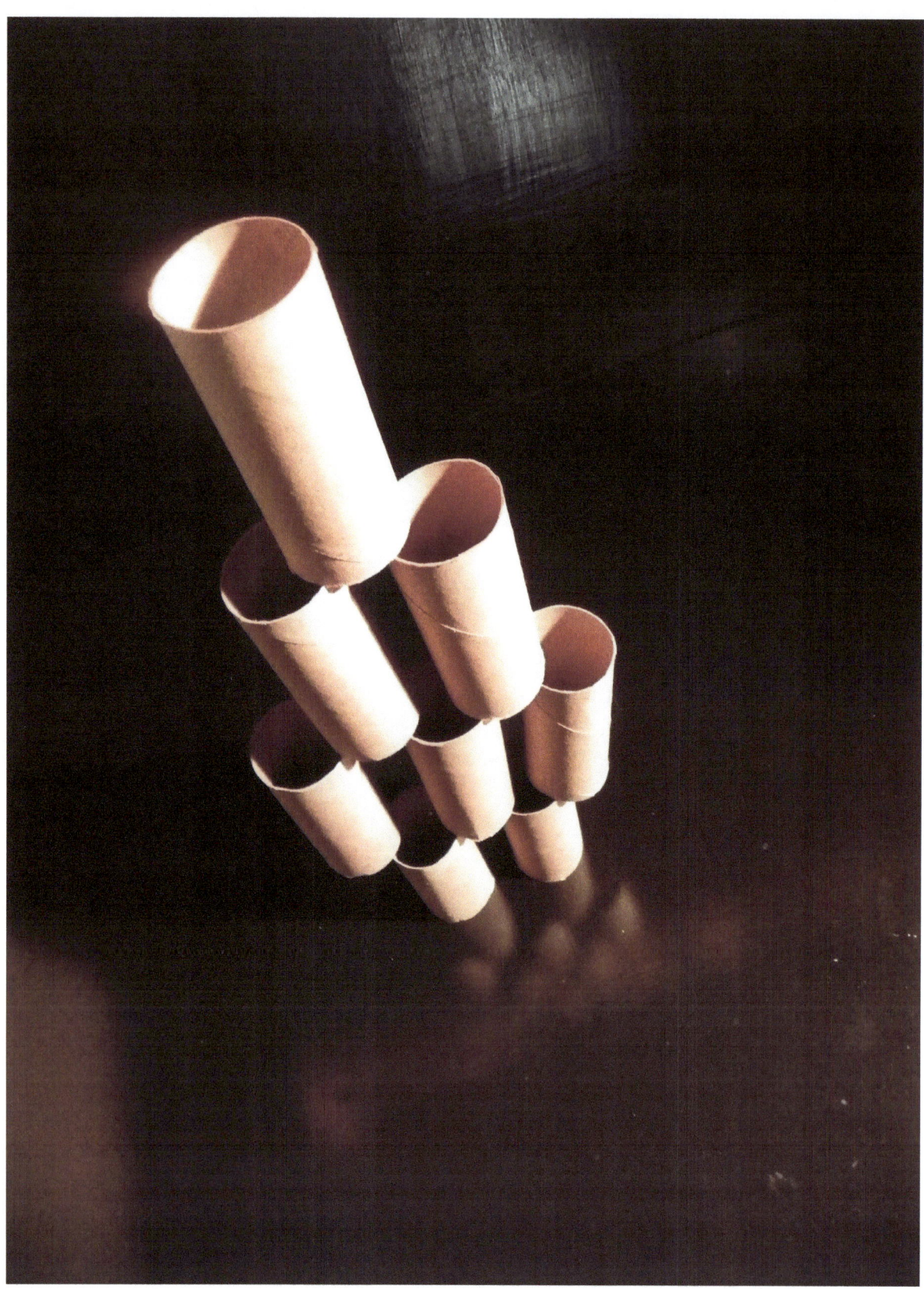

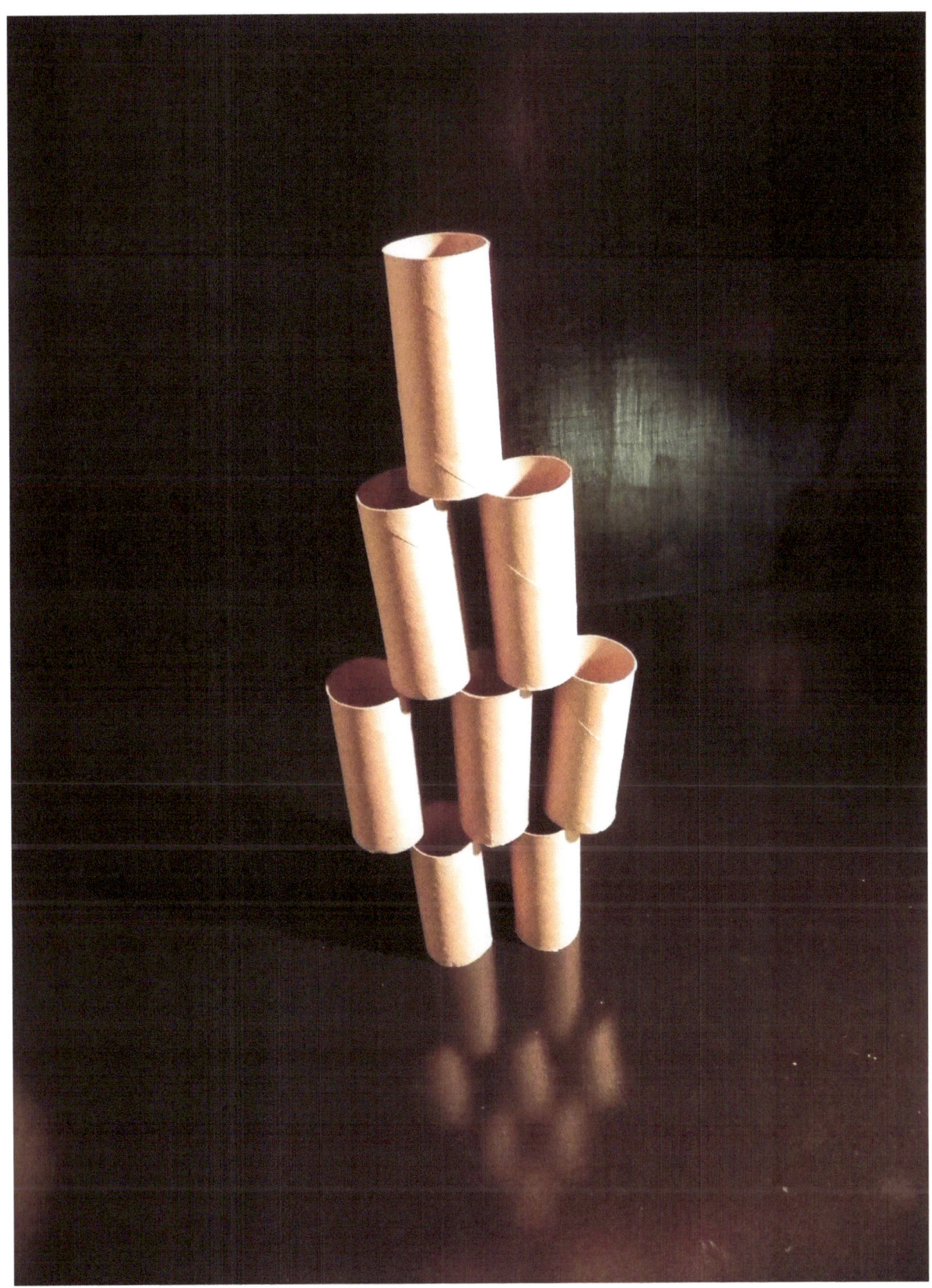

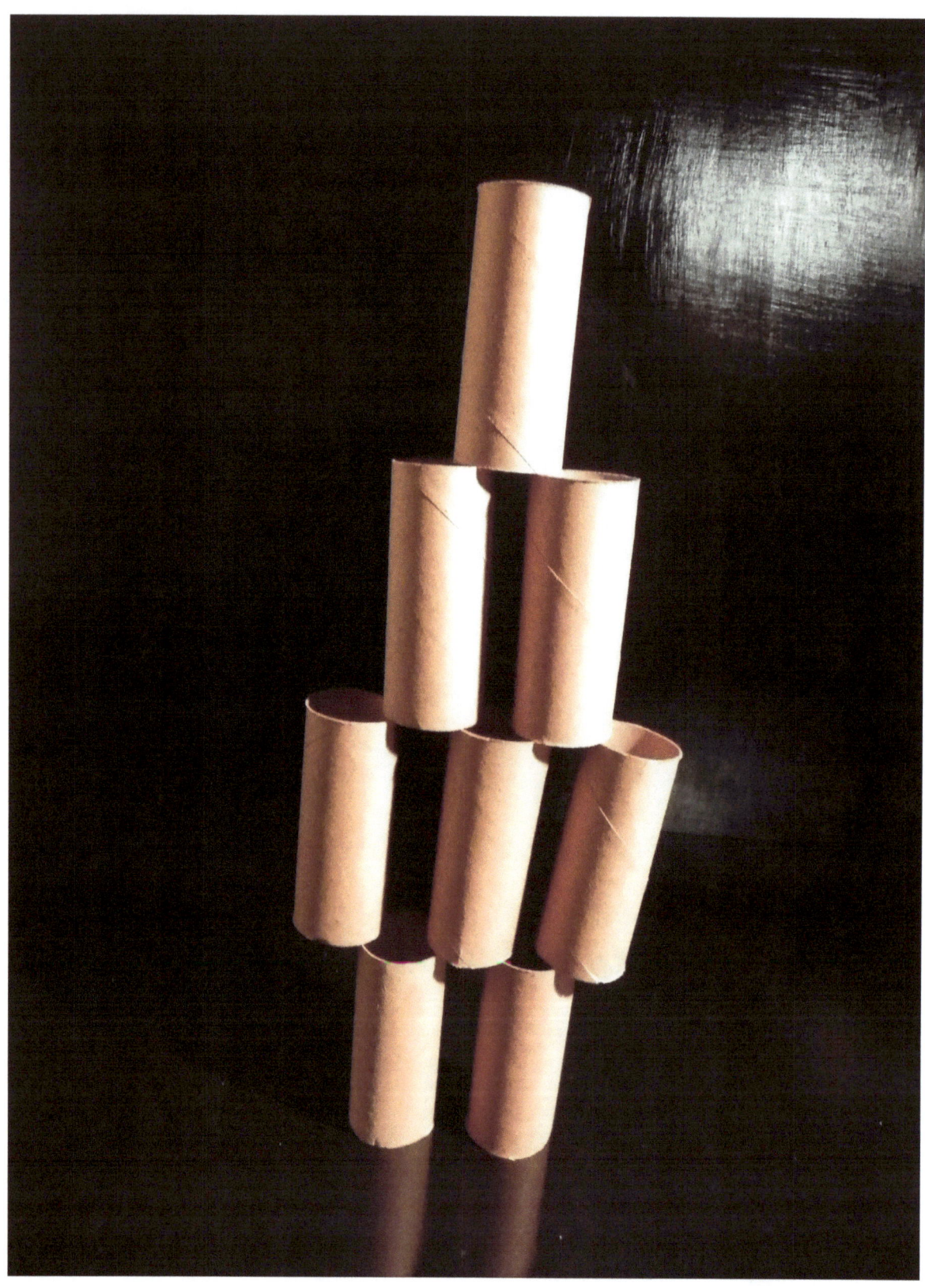

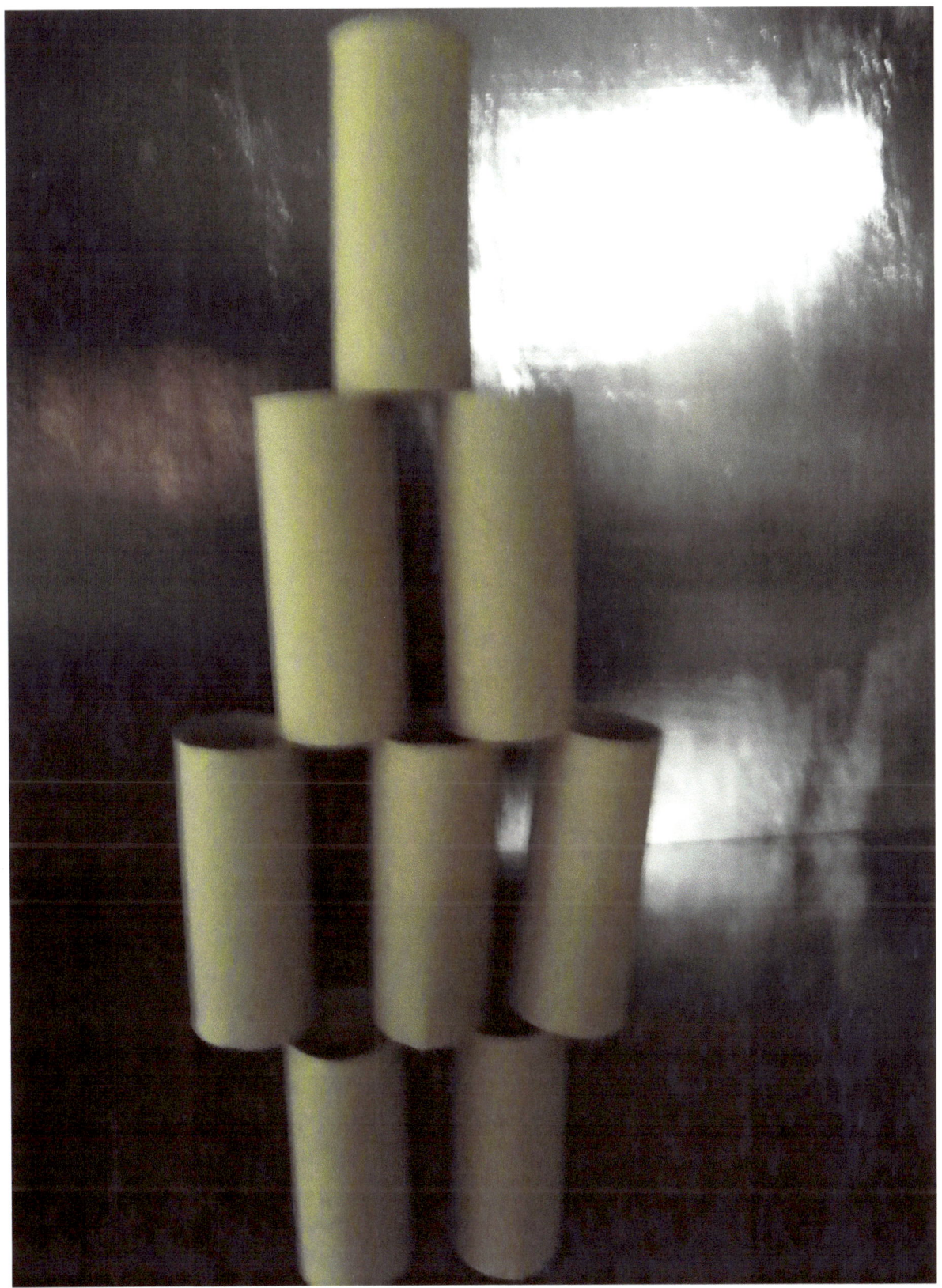

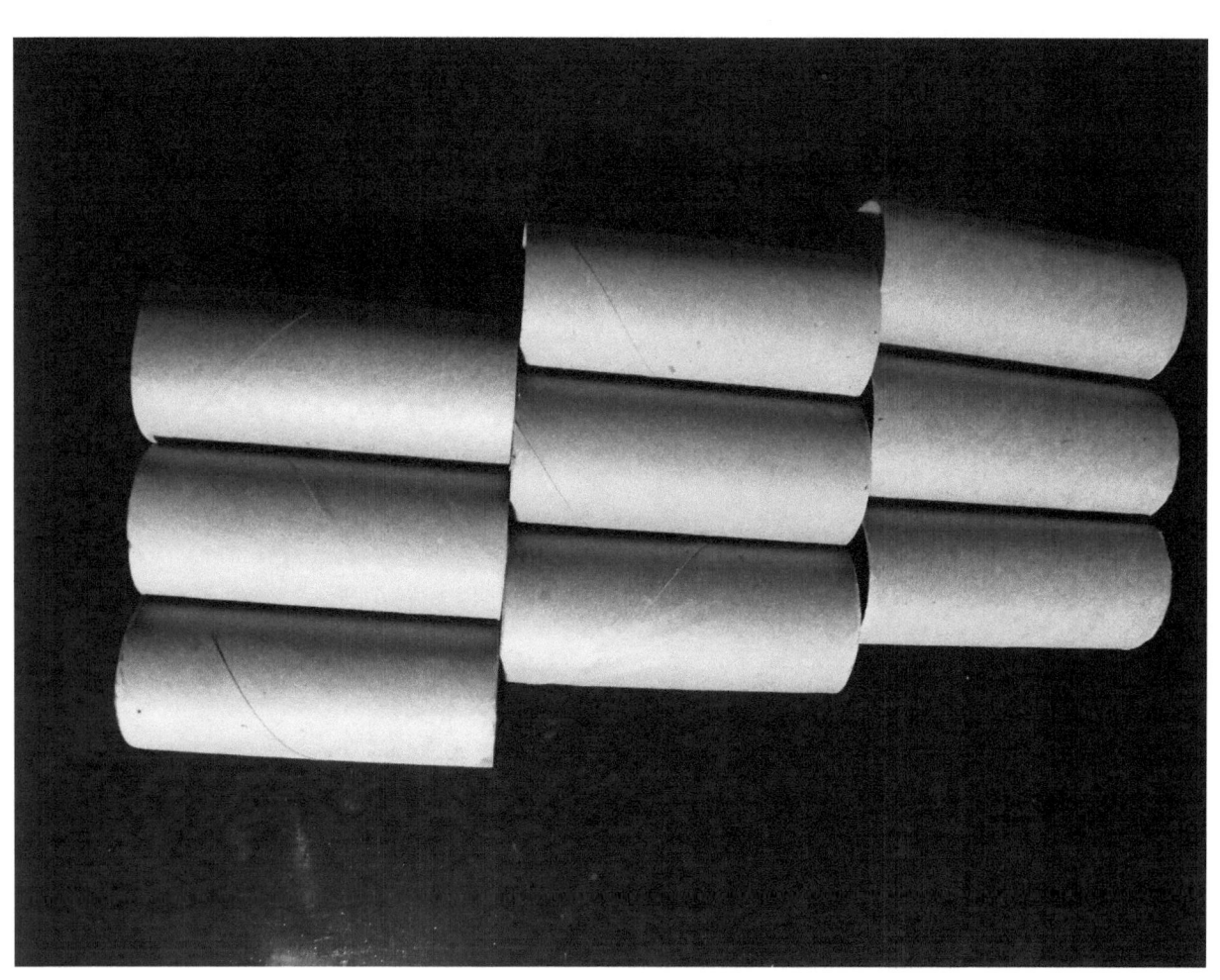

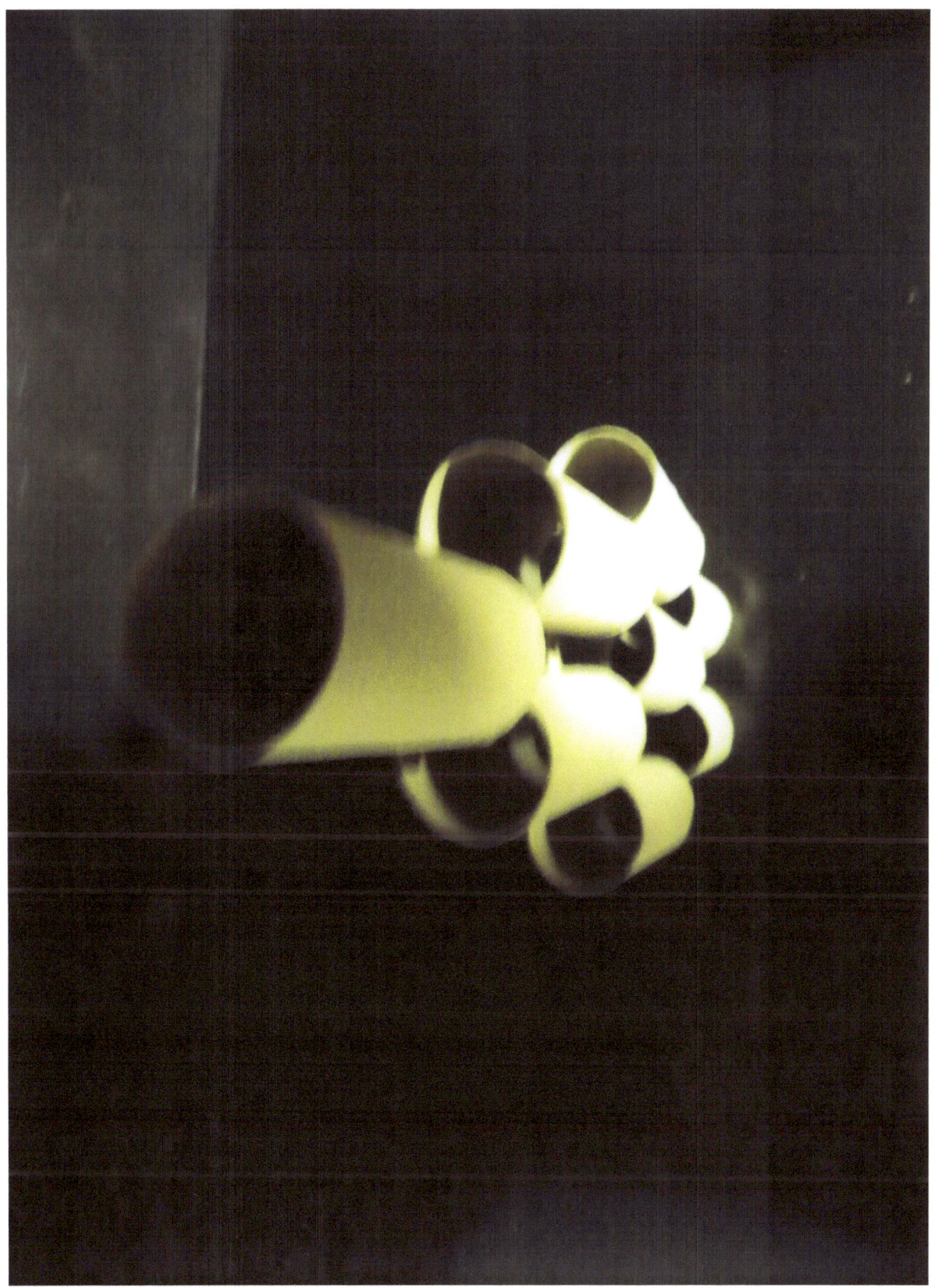

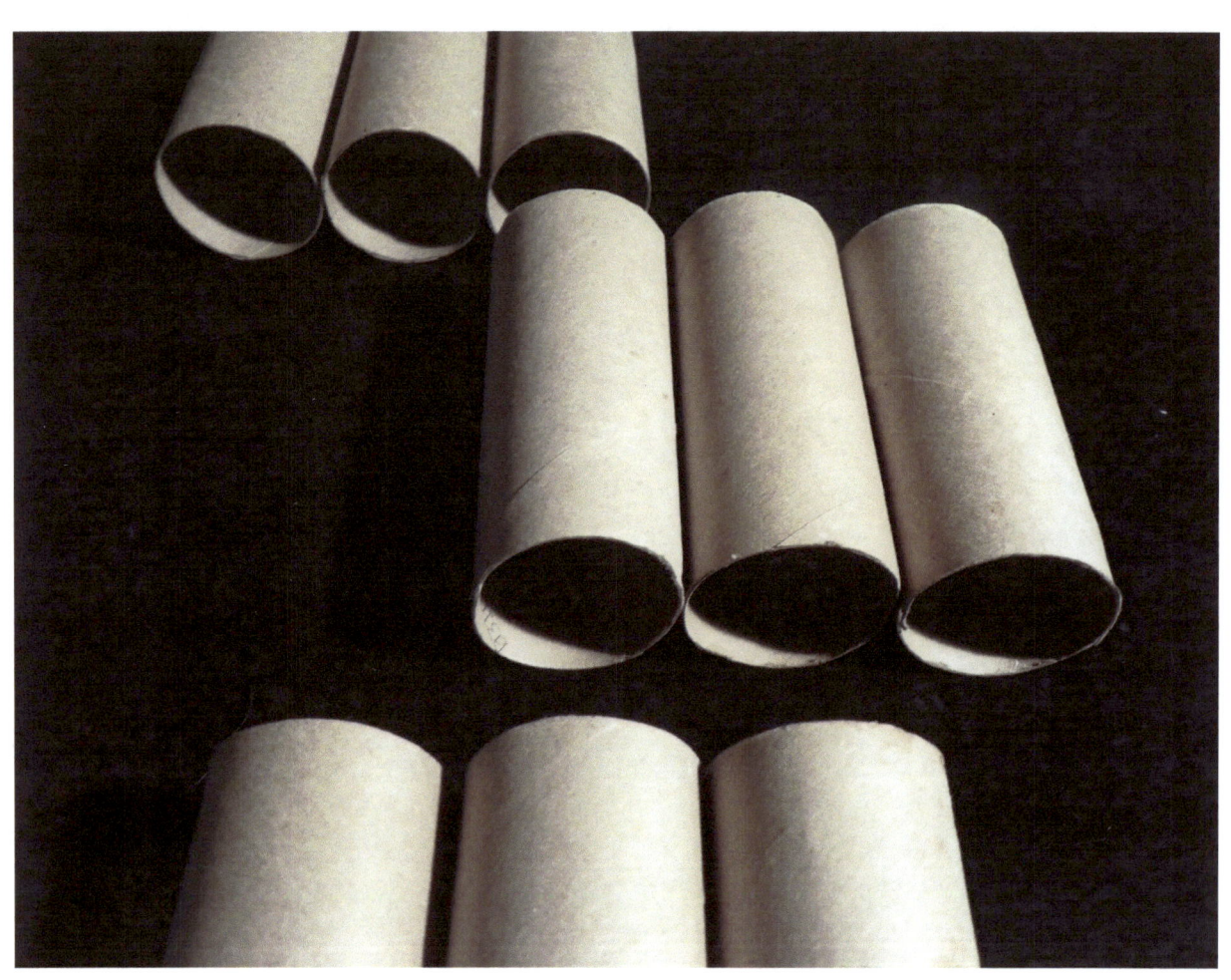

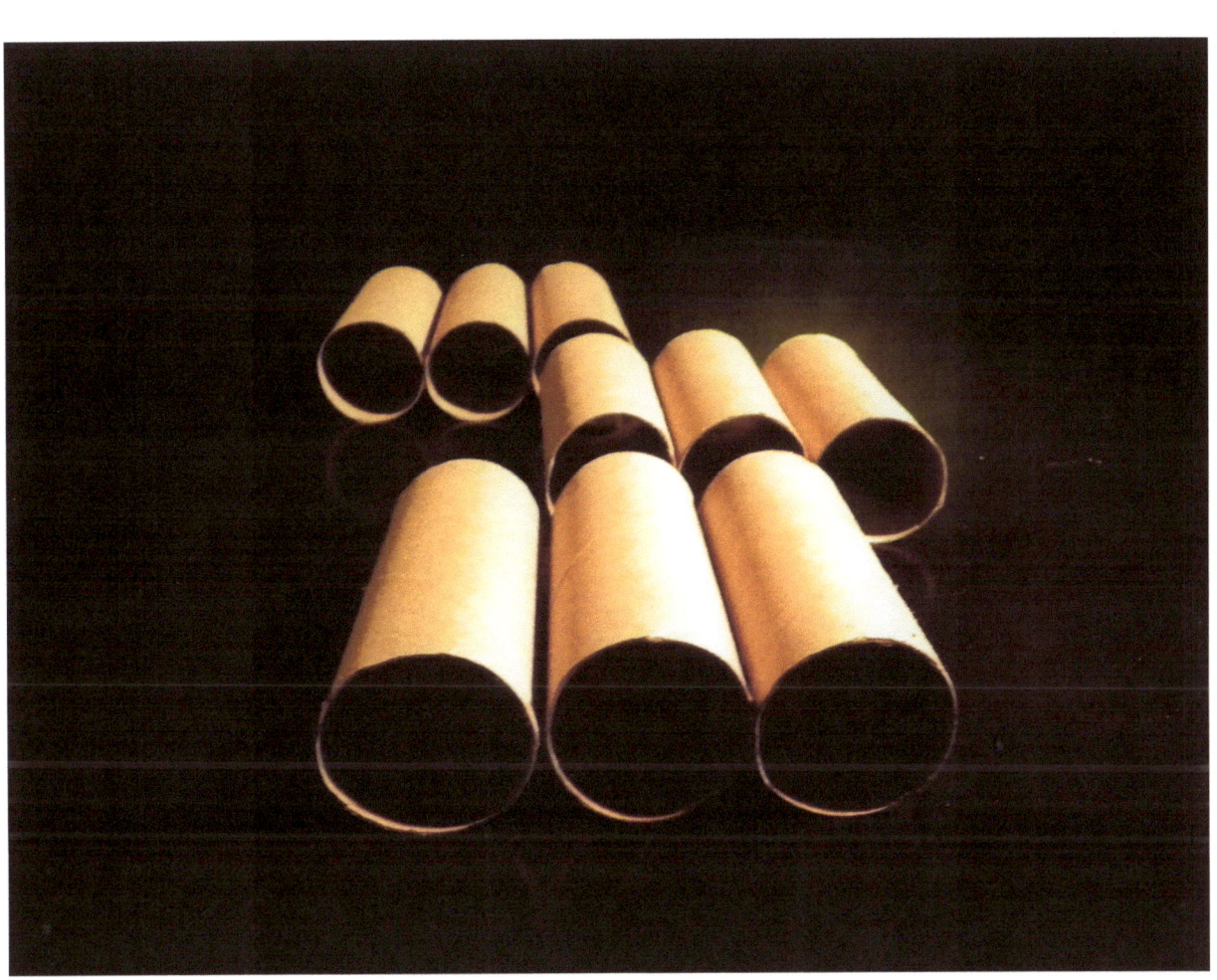

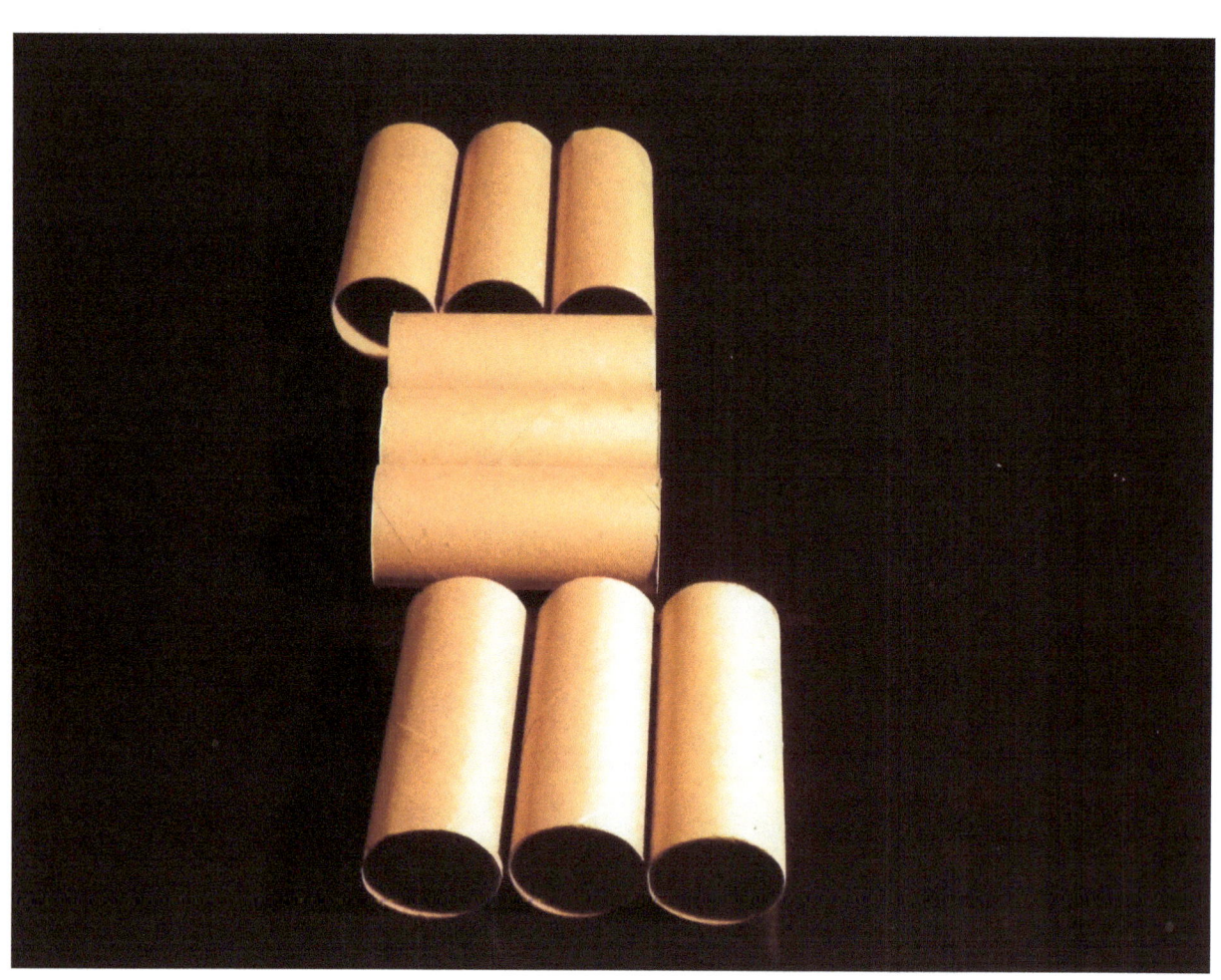

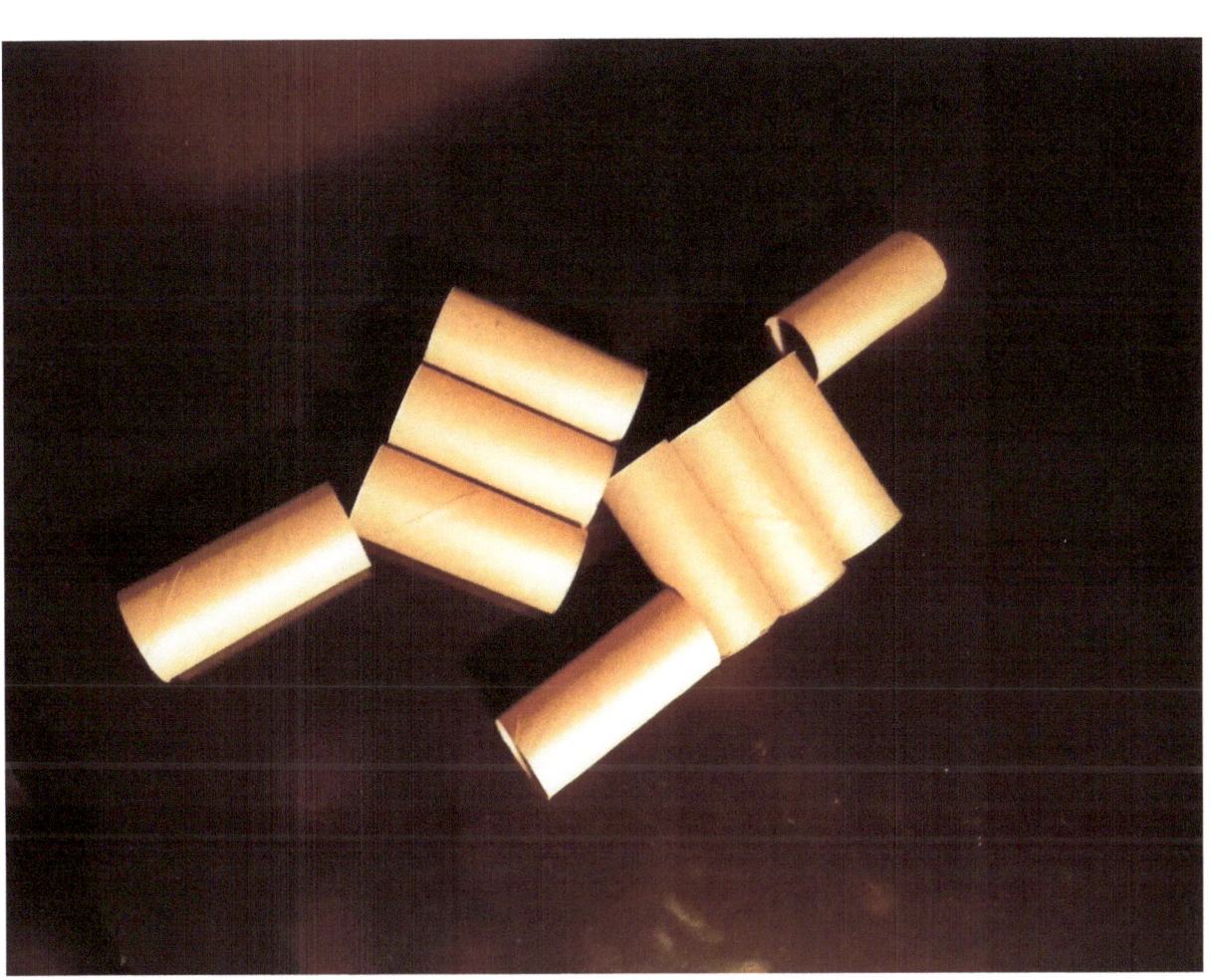

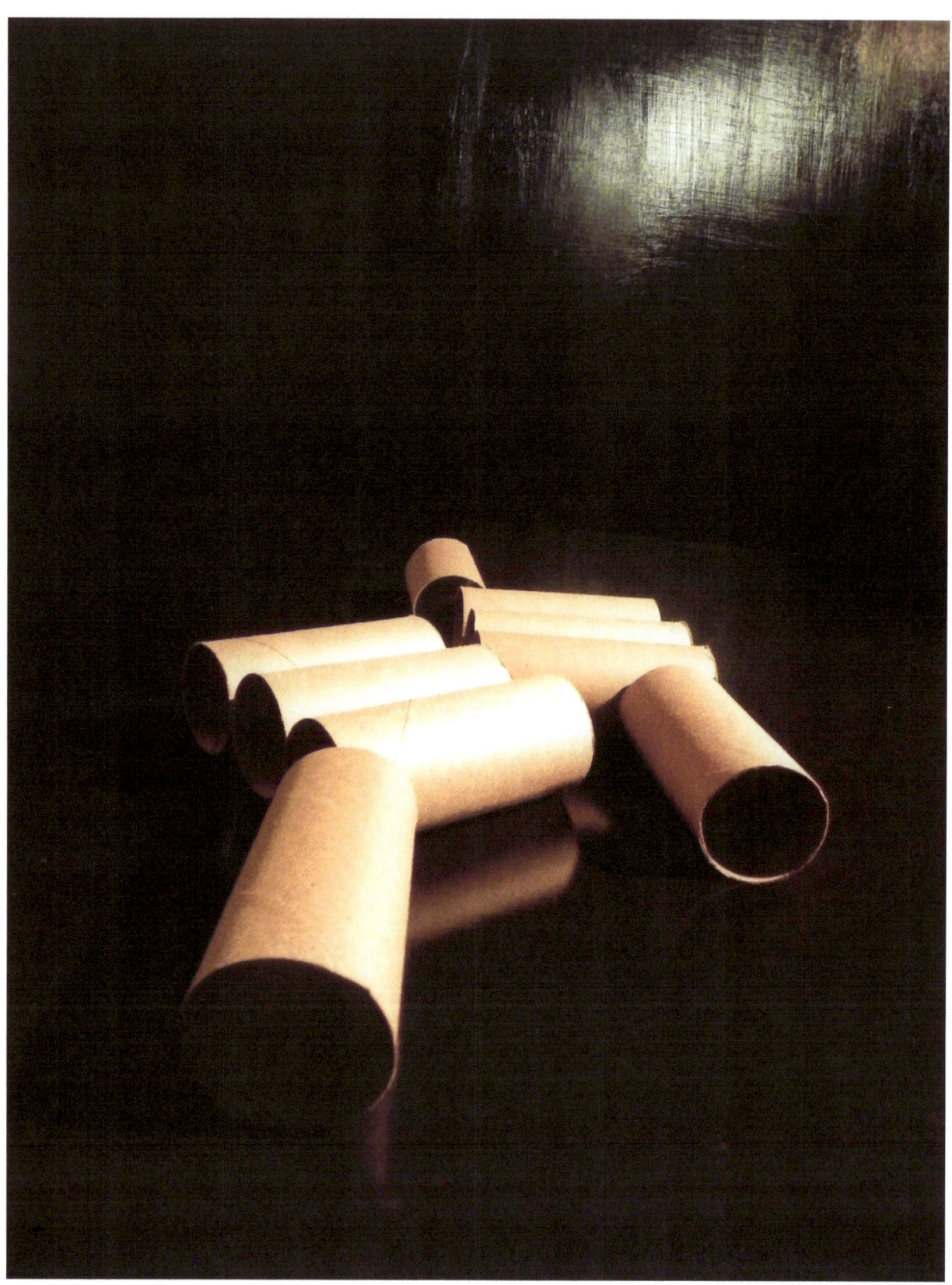

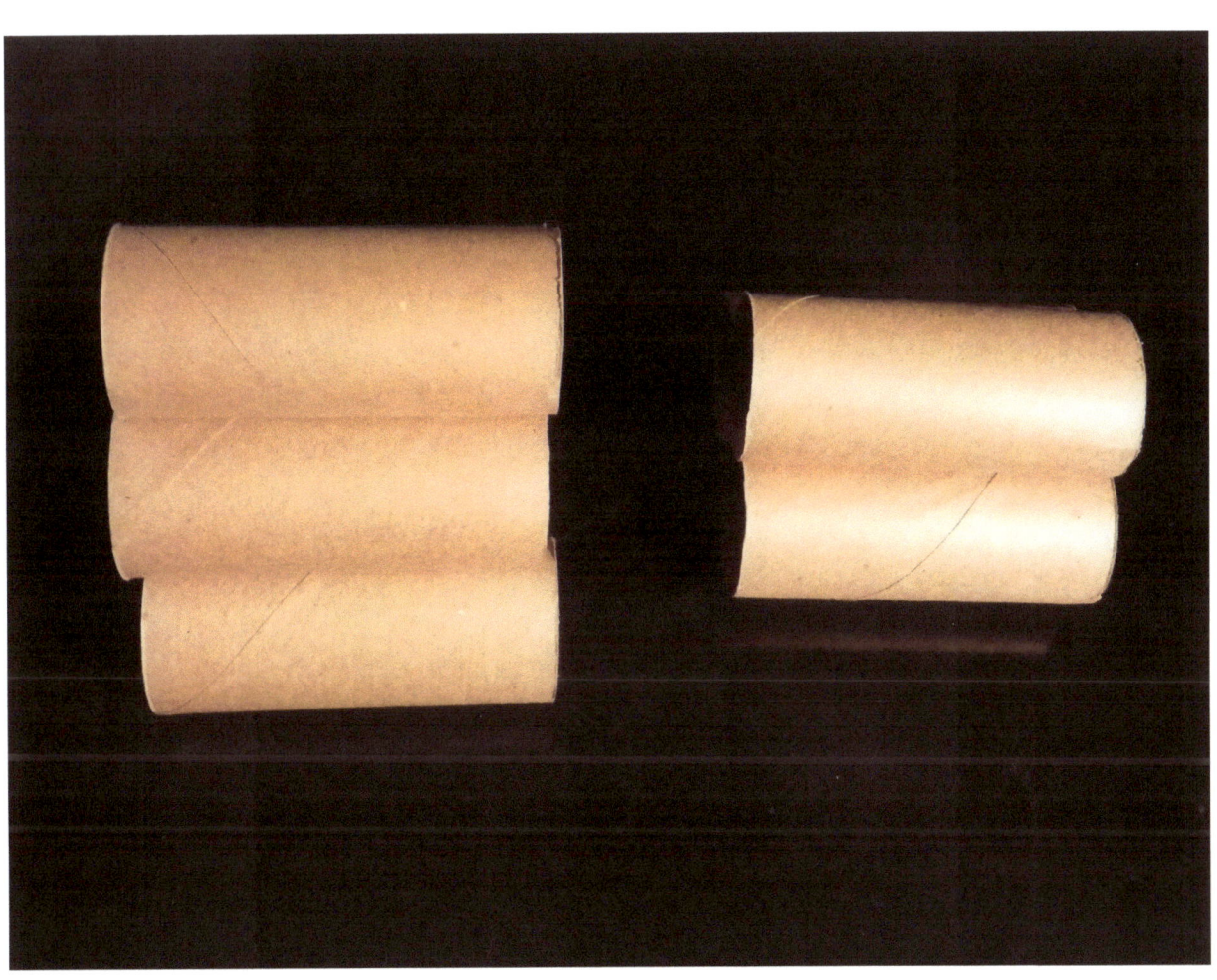

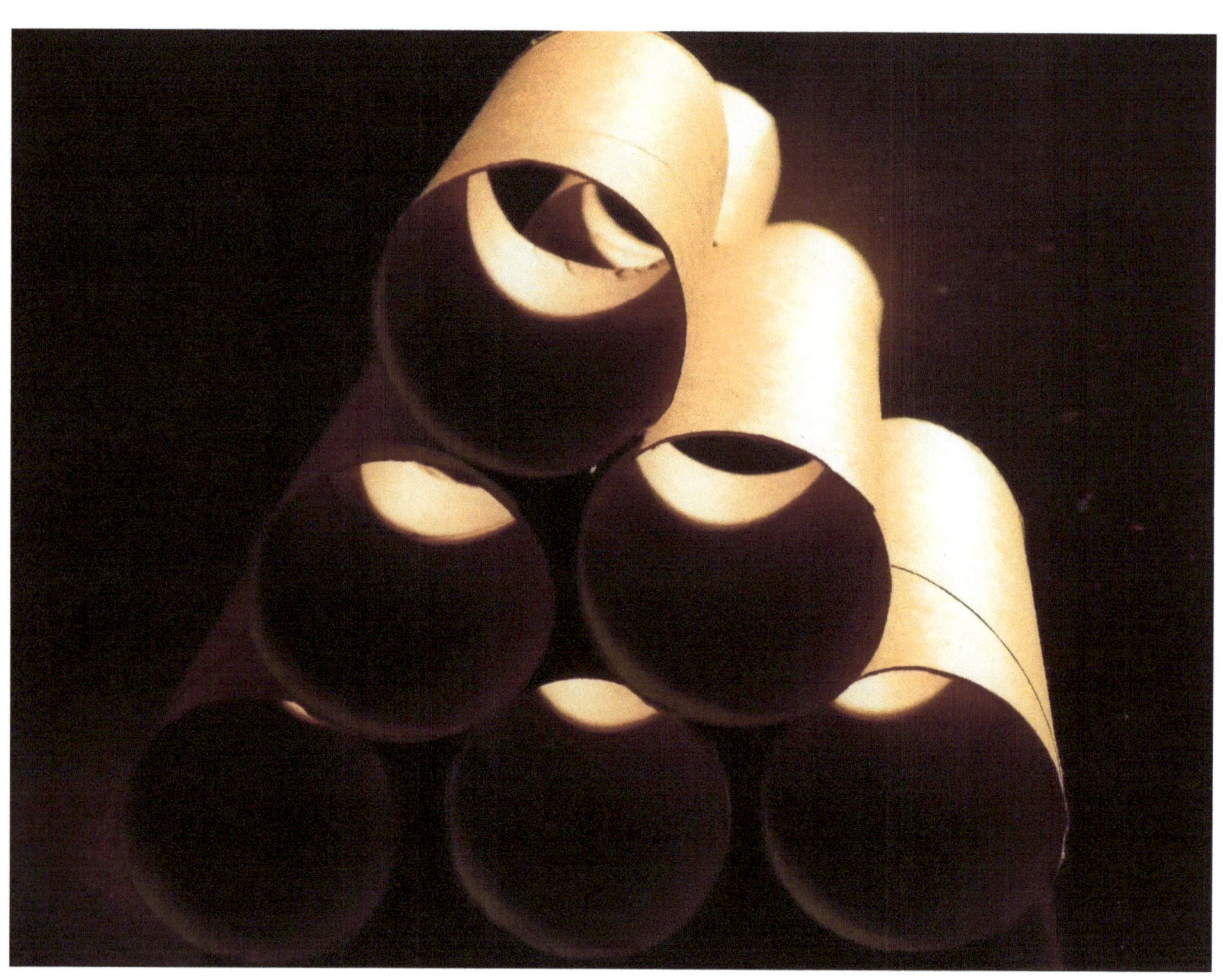

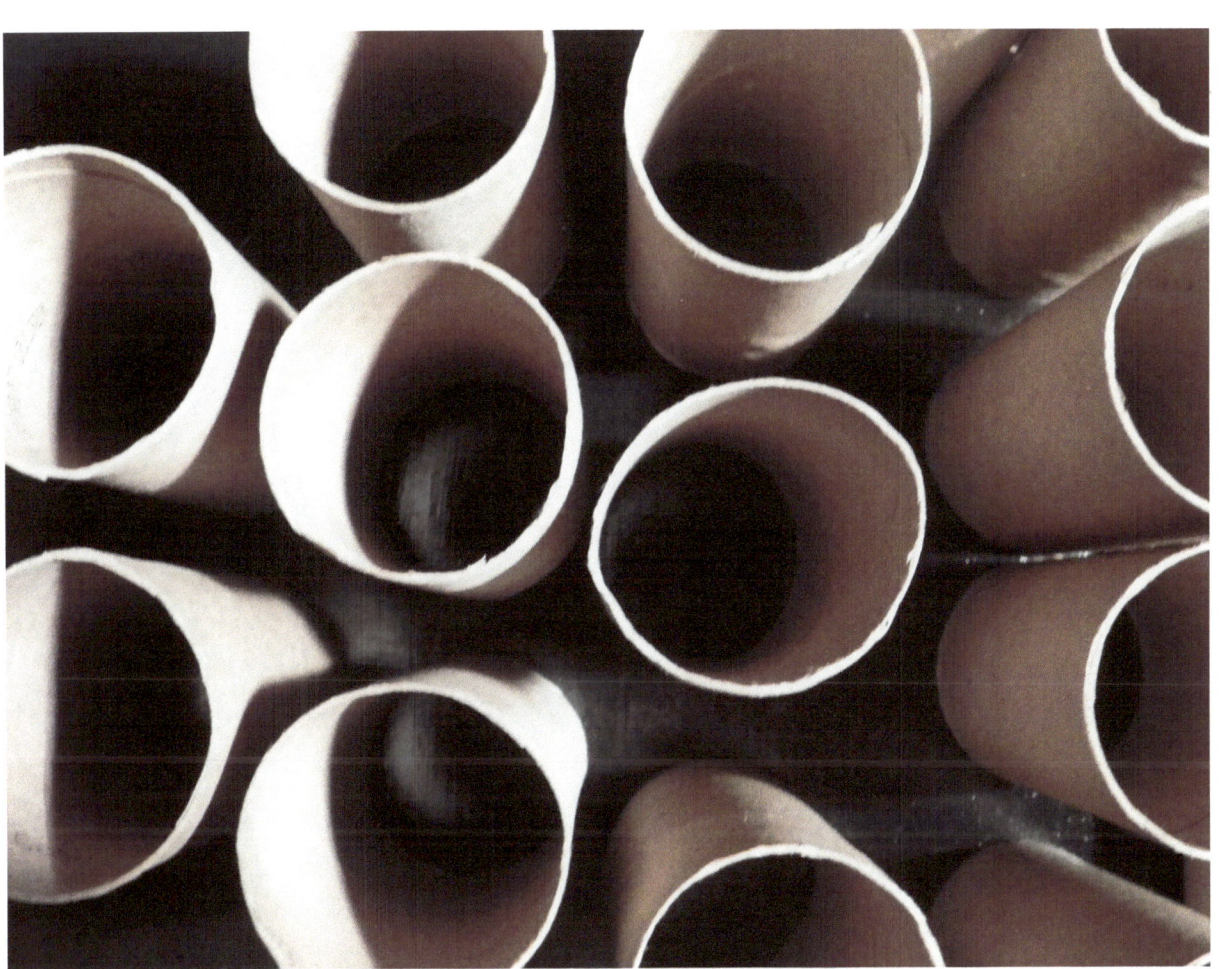

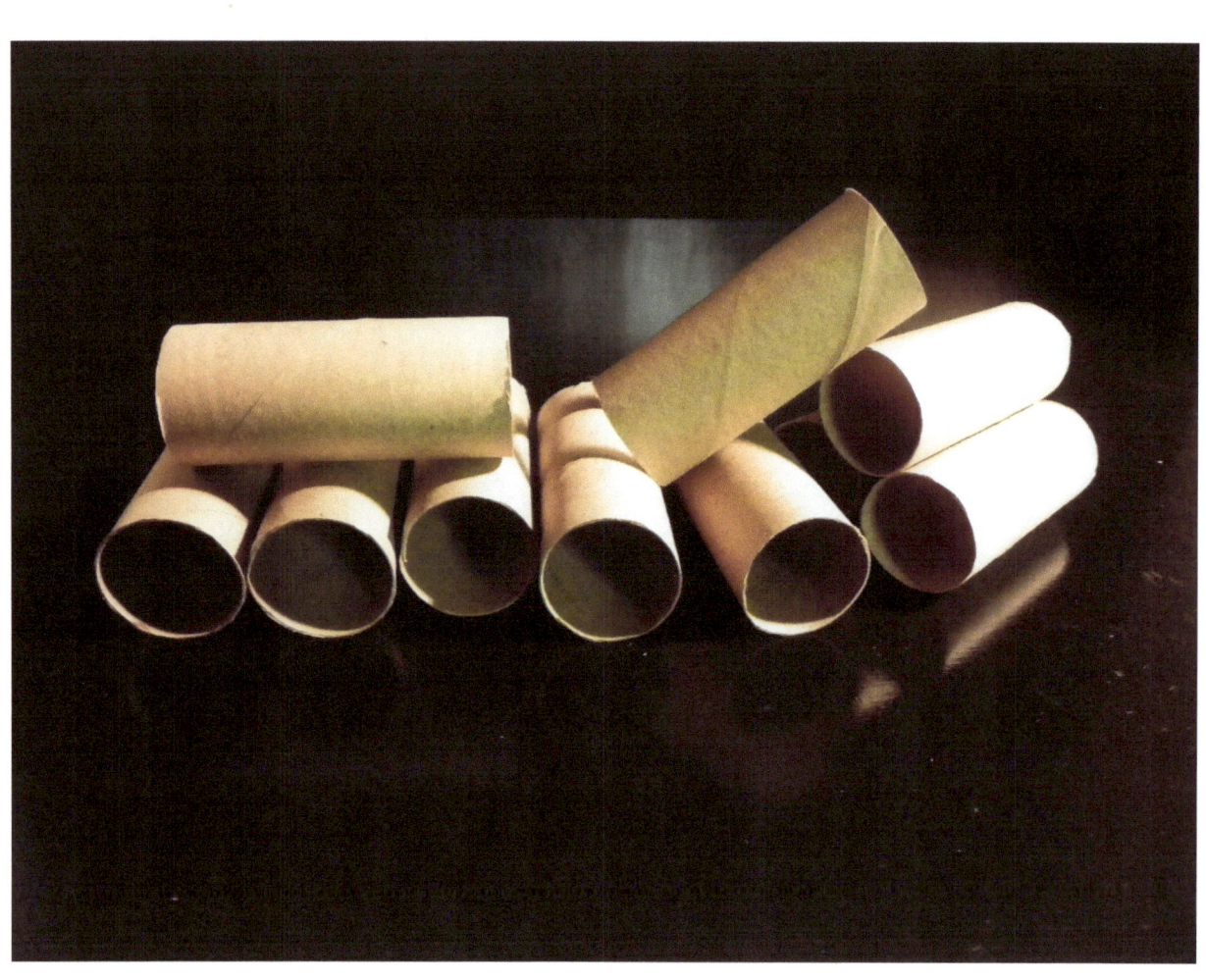

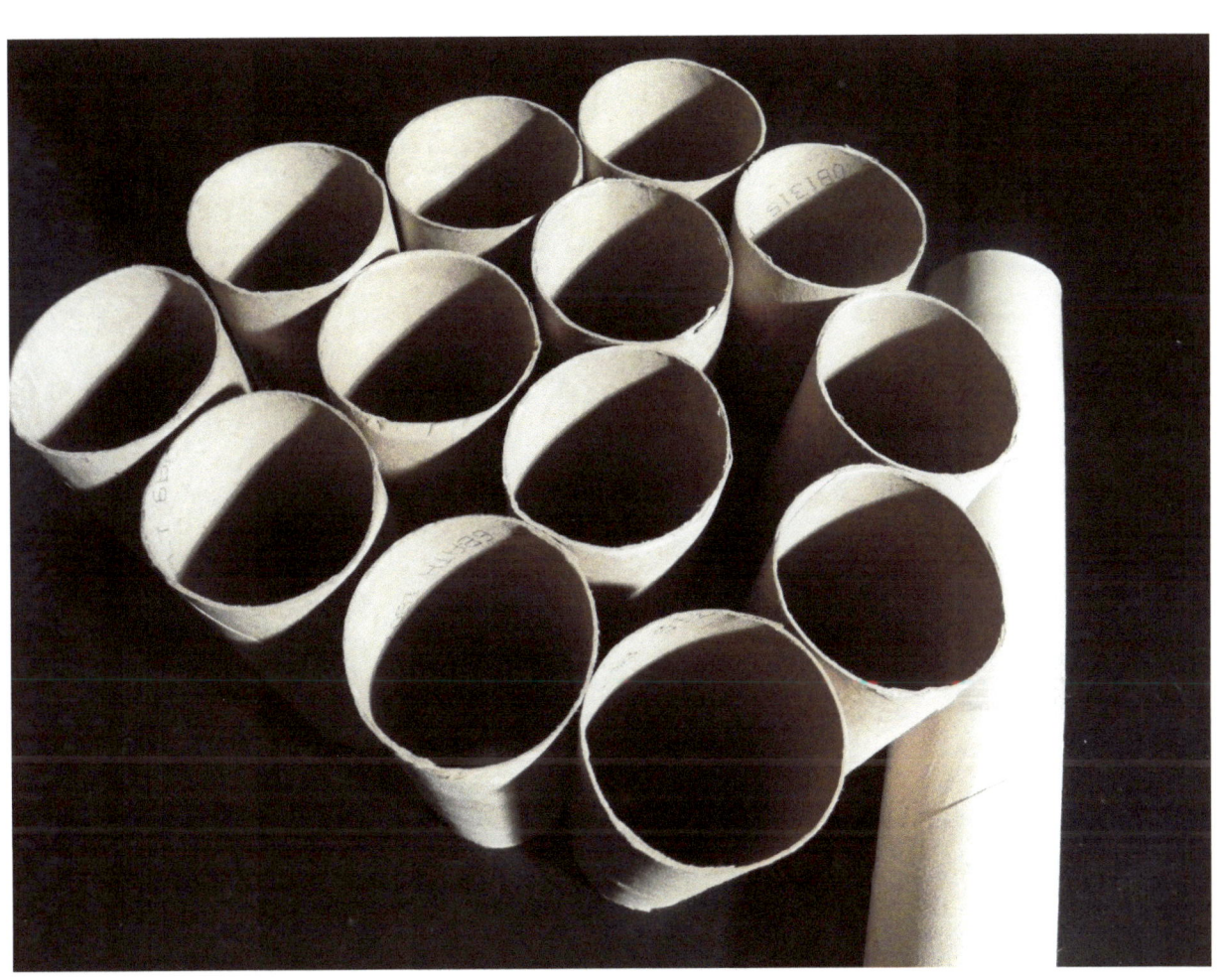

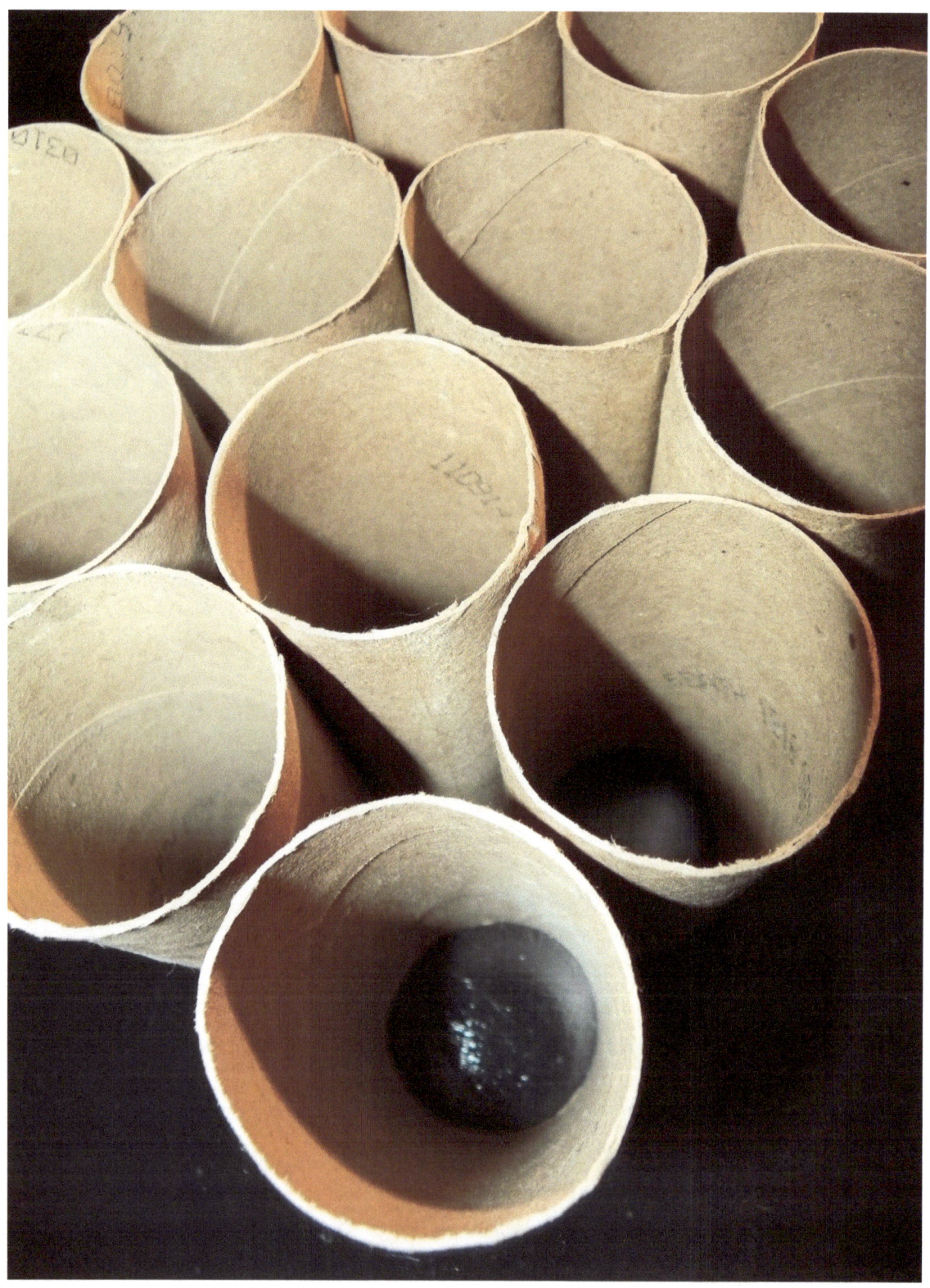

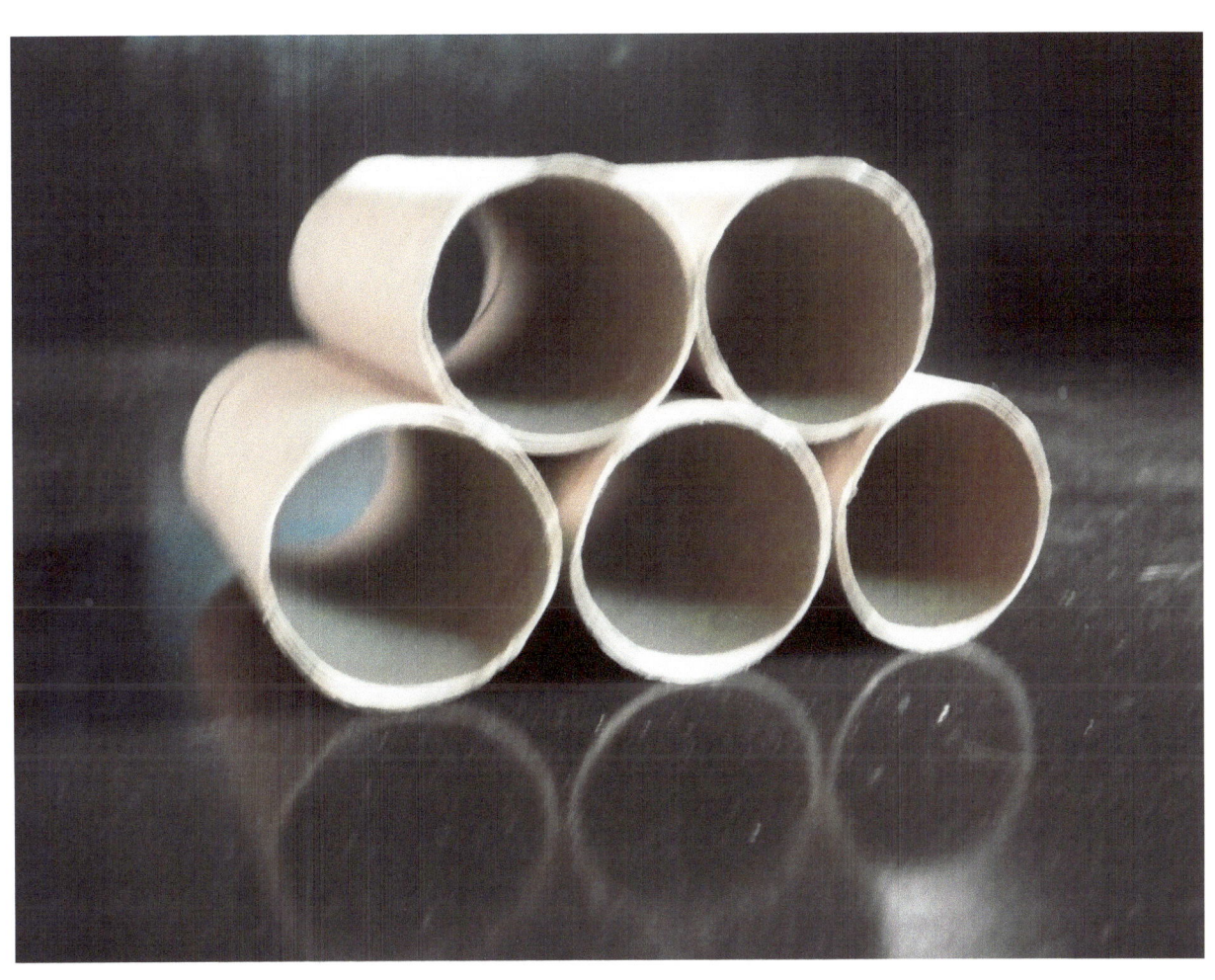

www.ingramcontent.com/pod-product-compliance
Lightning Source LLC
Chambersburg PA
CBHW051201220526
45473CB00003B/860